California

NATIONAL  FORESTS

National
Forests
— of —
America

Andrew Horan

ACKNOWLEDGMENTS

High in the Sierra Nevada, where the aroma of pine, fir, and incense-cedar mingle at dusk before drifting to tickle the glimmering stars, the glory of solitude and the joys of collaboration melded and seared my soul.

Special thanks to the Forest Service personnel who took a special interest in this book, just as they take a special interest in the land: Jean Hawthorne, Gerald Reponen, Rita Green, Melissa Hearst, Jon Silvius, Judi Downing, Dave McMorran, Dave Reider, Dave Jones, Jim Johnston, Alice Buckley, Molly McCartney, Carole Gerard, Bob McDowell, Richard Gibson, and Jeff Applegate.

Thanks also to editor Chris Cauble, for his guidance, and to publisher Bill Schneider.

ABOUT THE AUTHOR

Andrew Horan is a journalist who has written about environmental issues from Southern California, Chicago, and Washington, D.C. He is currently a staff reporter with the Orange County, Calif., *Register* and a freelance writer with articles in the Los Angeles *Reader* and *Outside* magazine. A backpacker and camper, Horan researched this book by visiting every national forest in California.

DEDICATION

To the shade of Robert Bailey Horan, Sr., who shouted John Cheever's words: "Fear tastes like a rusty knife, and do not let her into your house. Courage tastes of blood."

NATIONAL FORESTS OF AMERICA SERIES STAFF

Publishers: Michael S. Sample, Bill Schnieder
Editor: Christopher Cauble
Photo editor: Michael S. Sample, DD Dowden
Design: Steve Morehouse, DD Dowden
Electronic paste-up: DD Dowden
Cartography: Marita Martiniak, Steve Morehouse
Marketing director: Kelly Simmons
Design, typesetting and other prepress work by Falcon Press, Helena, Montana. Printed in Korea.

Front cover photo: Bill Evarts, giant sequoias, Sierra National Forest

Back cover photos: Jon Gnass, backpackers, Toiyabe National Forest; Larry Ulrich, skiers, Inyo National Forest; Michael S. Sample, mule deer; Roy Murphy, knobcone pine cones.

Title page photo: Bill Evarts, sequoia and mixed conifers, Sierra National Forest.

Published in cooperation with the Forest Service and the national forest interpretive associations of California.

Library of Congress Number 88-83880

ISBN 0-937959-59-6

For additional copies of this book, write to Falcon Press, P.O. Box 1718, Helena, MT 59624, or call toll free 1-800-582-BOOK.

*"National Forests
will be managed
for the greatest
good for the greatest
number of people in
the long run."*

Gifford Pinchot
First Chief of the Forest Service, 1905

GALEN ROWELL

> "National Forests serve a good purpose as playgrounds for people. They are used ... by campers, hunters, fishermen, and thousands of pleasure seekers from nearby towns. They are great recreation grounds for a large part of the people of the West, and their value in this respect is well worth considering."
>
> Gifford Pinchot
> First Chief of the Forest Service, 1907

CHARLES A. MAUZY

Contents

Santa Lucia Range from the coast at Pacific Valley, Los Padres National Forest. LARRY ULRICH

Introduction

National forests for everyone

From mighty Douglas-fir stands at the Oregon border south to ceanothus shrubs near Mexico, from Pacific Ocean beaches east to 4,700-year-old bristlecone pines rising above the Great Basin desert, the nineteen national forests in California cover twenty million acres—twenty percent of the state. These public lands attract more than sixty million visitors a year—ten times as many as Yosemite, Sequoia, and Kings Canyon national parks combined.

Visitors come to enjoy an almost limitless variety of outdoor recreation. California national forests contain more than 850 campgrounds—a third of the state's total—all linked by thousands of miles of scenic roads. Ten thousand miles of trails lure hikers, horseback riders, off-road vehicle drivers, mountain bicyclists, nordic skiers, and snowmobilers. Thirteen thousand miles of streams and rivers—and thousands of acres of lakes—beckon fishermen, kayakers, rafters, motorboaters, and houseboaters. Thirty-two major ski resorts operate over a hundred miles of downhill runs on national forest land.

Rock climbers flock to The Needles in Sequoia National Forest, one of the dozen best—and least crowded—series of climbing rocks in the country. Others scramble up Mt. Whitney, California's highest peak, in Inyo National Forest. Backpackers stream into the spectacular John Muir and Ansel Adams wilderness areas—two of the forty-six wilderness areas covering 3.9 million acres in California national forests. Hikers trek the Pacific Crest Trail that stitches through fourteen of these national forests. River runners gather in Stanislaus, Klamath, and Sequoia national forests—some of the top white-water areas in the nation—to sample some of the 1,800 miles of wild and scenic rivers that tumble through national forest canyons and valleys.

Fishermen cast for chinook and kokanee salmon, steelhead and rainbow trout, and thirty-one other species of fish in the streams and lakes of California national forests. Hunters track deer, bear, antelope, and quail—forty-six game animals all told—while bald eagles, Santa Ana River wooly stars, and thirty-eight other threatened or endangered plant and animal species inhabit national forest lands.

Along with all this, the national forests support timber, livestock, mining, and energy industries, and visitors may find themselves recreating on national forest lands where these uses are evident. Douglas-fir, sugar pine, ponderosa pine, and dozens of other conifer trees are harvested on nearly a fourth of the national forest lands, and California national forests produce more timber than all states except Washington and Oregon.

Almost half of the Golden State's drinking and irrigation water flows out of the national forests, much of it after pooling in 2,400 reservoirs behind dams that stem floods and generate electricity.

Miners dig gold, nickel, cobalt, copper, and uranium from under California national forests. Oil, natural gas—even hot springs—are tapped to fuel the state. Nearly 155,000 cattle, sheep, and horses graze on 4.5 million acres of national forest land.

These industries pay the Forest Service about $206 million a year. Of this amount, 25 percent—about $52 million each year—goes to local county governments for schools and roads.

Evidence of all this work and play—logging trucks, grazing cattle, busy campgrounds, pristine wilderness areas—comes as a shock to some forest visitors. Some expect national forests to be preserves like national parks. Others expect national forests to be outdoor factories. The real national forests operate by balancing these expectations.

National forests were created to stop the destructive "cut and run" practices of the 19th century. All across the country, virgin forest were cleared with saws

Fall's color highlights McGee Creek Valley in Inyo National Forest. ED COOPER

and fires to make room for farms and towns. In California, loggers cut stands of the Sierra Nevada and moved west under an ethic that assumed more woods would lie ahead forever. Hydraulic gold miners sprayed water onto mountain slopes with such force that the ground sloughed away, exposing cliffs that still stand naked today. Cattlemen and sheepherders grazed meadows and valleys until the grasslands turned to dust, then moved to the next pasture, assuming that another pasture always awaited them.

Early conservationists protested the destruction and called for protection. The federal government began setting aside forest reserves in 1891, and California led the way. Portions of today's Angeles, Los Padres, San Bernardino, Sierra, Eldorado, and Stanislaus national forests were among the first reserves created. In 1907 all reserves became national forests under the Forest Service in the U.S. Department of Agriculture.

Gifford Pinchot, the first chief of the Forest Service, defined the purpose of national forests when he published the pocket-size "use book" in 1905. The forty-page pamphlet instructed rangers, who then earned $1,400 a year, that "the timber, water, pastures, minerals, and other resources of the national forests are for the use of the people." Pinchot also noted that national forests served a good purpose as "recreation grounds."

Much has changed since then, and national forests continue to refine Pinchot's early vision. Along with timber harvesting and other commercial uses, outdoor recreation is increasingly important as millions of Americans seek the last remaining open spaces. As a result, national forests are refurbishing campgrounds, installing wheelchair access to trails and lakes, conducting interpretive programs, designating scenic byways, and providing more outlets for the tremendous variety of outdoor recreation that visitors enjoy.

Nowhere is this variety more evident than in the national forests of California. ∎

E X P E R T S I N M A N Y F I E L D S

When the Forest Service was created in 1905, its first chief, Gifford Pinchot, organized the agency to provide local forest officials with authority over daily and long-term decisions. That basic organization still holds true, but national forests now face complex decisions that Pinchot never could have foreseen. As a result, today's national forests depend on experts in many fields.

Direct responsibility for each national forest falls on the shoulders of a forest supervisor. Next come the district rangers, each responsible for his or her district within the national forest. Then, depending on the needs of each national forest, there are foresters, recreation technicians, wilderness rangers, archaeologists, historians, hydrologists, firefighters, computer programmers, soil scientists, landscape architects, wildlife biologists, botanists, personnel administrators, public information officers, entomologists, writers and editors, and timber specialists to name a few. (In this book, California National Forests, the term "forester" is used in a general sense to indicate a Forest Service employee. However, in a strict sense, a

forester is a professional trained in the management of forested lands in any of several disciplines.)

In all, California national forests employ about 5,800 full-time workers. In the summer, the ranks swell with another 2,700

A Forest Service biologist instructs a college biology class.
TOM MYERS

The Forest Service shield has been the symbol of the Forest Service since 1905.

temporary employees who fight fires, staff fire-lookout towers, and conduct recreation programs. Thousands of volunteers lend their support by cutting and maintaining trails and working in visitors' centers.

*Sturtevant Falls is one of dozens of waterfalls that surprise thirsty tourists by
tumbling out of Angeles National Forest's Big Santa Anita Canyon.* ROY MURPHY

Angeles, Cleveland, and San Bernardino

Holding back the big city

The Angeles, San Bernardino, and Cleveland national forests are among the smallest in California, but they attract more visitors than all other national forests in the state. Their popularity is partly due to their location—they wrap around almost eighteen million people living in more than one hundred Southern California towns. To these smog-bound city dwellers, the national forests offer clean air, bright skies, and clear water—appealing outdoor attributes that lure fifty million visitors a year.

Squeezed by Southern California's expanding population, these three national forests serve other purposes besides recreation. Their chaparral brush and high-elevation conifers strain to cleanse the area's polluted air, and nine forest rivers provide about twenty percent of Southern California's water.

Ten multi-lane freeways loop around and through the three national forests, and thousands of homes in five of the state's fastest-growing counties abut forest boundaries. New housing developments crowd into canyons on all sides. Coyotes and mountain lions occasionally wander into back yards, and, at times, fires, floods, and landslides sweep across property boundaries.

All of this activity takes place on some of the youngest and strangest mountains in California. All of Angeles National Forest and the northern part of San Bernardino National Forest lie on Transverse Ranges, the state's only major mountains that run east-west. The Cleveland National Forest and the southern portion of San Bernardino encompass Peninsular Ranges, rocky peaks that form the spine of the Baja Peninsula. Both the

Transverse and Peninsular ranges contain unstable rock that frequently sloughs off the steep slopes, especially after an intense rain.

While the mountains are relatively young, southern California forest history is relatively old. Parts of what would become the three national forests were designated as federal timberland reserves in the 1890s, more than a decade before Congress created the Forest Service. Presidents Benjamin Harrison, Grover Cleveland, and Theodore Roosevelt set aside the reserves and forests to curb wasteful timber cutting and control fires that threatened watersheds to the burgeoning towns below.

The towns grew larger than any of the early settlers could have imagined. With more people crowding the valleys and foothills, the Angeles, San Bernardino, and Cleveland national forests now protect southern California's last—and best—open spaces.

Chaparral-covered San Dimas Experimental Forest, where researchers study the impact of smog on the ability of soils and plants to gather and hold water, unfolds below Johnstone Peak in the Angeles National Forest.
ROY MURPHY

ANGELES
N A T I O N A L F O R E S T

Divided into two sections on the Sierra Pelona and San Gabriel mountains, the Angeles National Forest appears to block—with declining success—Los Angeles as it sprawls to the north.

The forest's mountains form a more effective climatic barrier, trapping Mediterranean weather along the coast and warding off the Mojave Desert to the northeast. The Los Angeles basin averages fourteen inches of rain a year, but the highest points of Angeles National Forest get almost sixty inches, mostly snow. Forest temperatures range from 110 in the summer to 10 below in the winter—surprising extremes just an hour's drive from temperate Pacific Ocean beaches.

The forest also stands between the city and the mighty San Andreas Fault, but the forest's multiple mountain ridges and 6,000- to 10,000-foot peaks will offer little protection from "The Big One," a massive earthquake expected to rumble along the fault sometime before

the year 2020.

In the meantime, Angeles National Forest provides a recreational outlet for millions of Southern Californians. Hikers explore three small, remote wilderness areas (San Gabriel, Sheep Mountain, and Cucamonga), but most visitors do what Southern Californians do best—they drive. The forest's scenic roads are among the most popular in California.

It may take a hiker patient observation to spot one of the 700 Nelson bighorn sheep in the Angeles' backcountry, but in just a few hours, motorists can marvel at streams, waterfalls, blossoming wildflowers, and aromatic conifers. Most travel occurs on nine forest roads—the Angeles Crest Highway, Angeles Forest Highway, San Gabriel Canyon Road, Glendora Ridge Road, Big Tujunga Canyon Road, Mt. Baldy Road,

Bouquet Creek Road, San Francisquito Road, and Little Tujunga Road.

These roads lead to three visitors' centers, six ski slopes, three off-road vehicle areas with 360 miles of existing and planned ORV routes, eleven target shooting sites, a dozen self-guided nature trails, 140 campground and picnic sites, and innumerable scenic vistas.

Two of the roads—Angeles Crest and San Gabriel Canyon—draw the bulk of traffic. The Angeles Forest Highway also is heavily traveled.

A less traveled road, the Old Ridge Route provides a two-hour, twenty-mile journey on the same sight-seeing road used by early travelers in Model A Fords. The route begins at the Los Angeles County Fire Station near Bald Mountain, where signs warn that maximum speed on the road is fifteen miles per hour and that road maintenance ends in half a mile. The road's original concrete pavement was laid in 1915 and remains in remarkably firm shape. Asphalt was later used to widen the road and straighten some of its sharp curves. In several areas, landslides have buried both surfaces under a foot or more of rock and dirt. The resulting bumps delight explorers with four-wheel drives, and, with caution, even a family car can navigate the road.

The route rewards careful drivers. Yucca and rabbitbrush bloom on the steep slopes above the road, while the wooded slopes of Liebre Mountain and the rusty-colored, twisted crags of Red Mountain dominate the eastern view. To the west, Pyramid Lake—popular for boating, fishing, and swimming—glints in the sun. Travelers can continue either north to Pyramid Lake or south to the main body of the forest and the communities of Los Angeles.

San Gabriel Canyon Road (Highway 39) is one of the busiest routes into Angeles National Forest. The road is wider and better maintained than the Old Ridge Route, and it attracts an estimated 15,000 to 20,000 people in 5,000 to 6,000 cars each weekend.

Many of the visitors drive eight miles to the San Gabriel off-road vehicle area, where pickup trucks, jeeps, and all-terrain vehicles make rooster-tailing runs across the muddy north shore of San Gabriel Reservoir. Hundreds of spectators with cameras, lawn chairs, and barbecue supplies gather on slopes above the reservoir to watch the ORV action below them.

From nearby Rincon Station, on-road vehicles can travel ninety minutes to the base of 10,064-foot Mt. San Antonio—known locally as Mt. Baldy—the highest peak in Angeles National Forest. The area supports a rustic village and downhill ski resort.

Although freeways circle the national forest and provide fast access to several forest recreation areas, one of the most popular drives remains the two-lane Angeles Crest Highway (Highway 2). The road winds through the forest's interior and takes travelers past numerous scenic views, campgrounds, picnic areas, and the national forest's Chilao Visitor Center.

Chilao Visitor Center provides water, rest, and information for thousands of travelers each month. Four short, self-guided nature walks begin at the center and teach about Native Americans, birds, wildlife, and forest history. One display features the first Forest Service cabin built in California. When fully restored, the one-room cabin will recreate historical features appropriate for its construction in 1900.

Summer visitors on the Angeles Crest Highway often seek cool woods and waters, such as Sturtevant Falls, the Mt. Islip area, and Buckhorn campground on Buckhorn Creek, where firs, incense cedars, and Jeffrey pines provide shade and beauty.

In the winter, skiers travel the highway for downhill skiing at Mt. Waterman and Kratka Ridge about ten miles east of Chilao, and at Mountain High East, Mountain High West, and Ski Sunrise near the Big Pines Recreation Area. Along the way, skiers pass Mt. Baden-Powell, named for Lord Baden-Powell who founded the Boy Scouts. The 9,399-foot peak provides a hostile home to twisted, tough, 2,000-year-old limber pines.

Big Pines Recreation Area is popular all year. A self-guided, two-hour auto trip takes drivers to lifts, sags, and scars that illustrate the powerful ripping and wrenching along the San Andreas Fault. Jackson Lake offers swimming and fishing in the summer, while cross-country ski trails lace the area in the winter.

A LABORATORY AS BIG AS A FOREST

Its two steep canyons look like most other canyons in Angeles National Forest, but the 32-square-mile San Dimas Experimental Forest serves a special purpose. Since 1935, scientists have measured stream flows, rainfall, vegetation growth, and animal behavior in San Dimas to get a better grasp on how a forest works.

Studies range from the mundane to the futuristic. The four hundred rainfall gauges scattered throughout the area,

which is off-limits to the public, don't elicit much excitement. But hundreds of scientists drew international attention in late 1986 and early 1987 when a portion of the experimental forest was set ablaze to reduce the risk of wildfire and study the ''nuclear winter'' hypothesis. The theory holds that smoke from nuclear weapons explosions would block the sun and create an era of deadly arctic weather.

The San Dimas and Big Dalton canyons

were drafted into the experimental forest in 1935 after lobbying by local scientists and the Los Angeles Chamber of Commerce, which was hoping to find a better way to hold water in the area and thus attract more settlers. One of the first experiments was to install special instruments under a variety of trees and shrubs to study how much water they transpire back into the air. Work continues today to determine how various plants hold soils and react to pollution.

The San Gabriel Mountains of the Angeles National Forest rise to 10,000 feet, trapping moist marine air in inversion layers over Los Angeles and blocking the southward advance of the high desert. DEDE GILMAN

As viewed from Angeles National Forest, the Los Angeles basin, above, spreads across five counties and harbors more than 13 million people.
ROB BADGER

Each year, national forest employees, right, at Crystal Lake Ranger Station in the Angeles National Forest lead thousands of children and adults from the busy streets of Los Angeles on contemplative nature walks. ROY MURPHY

SAN BERNARDINO

San Bernardino is the most Sierra-like national forest in Southern California. Mt. San Gorgonio, the highest point in Southern California, rises 11,499 feet above sea level. Tahquitz Peak and Suicide Rock in the San Jacinto Wilderness east of Riverside offer the best rock climbing in this part of the state. Steep slopes are heavily forested with old stands of lodgepole, Jeffery, ponderosa, and sugar pine, white fir and Douglas-fir, and California black and live oaks.

The bulk of San Bernardino National Forest lies east of Cajon Pass, a windy dip on Interstate 15 where the San Andreas Fault zips through to mark the end of the San Gabriel Range and the beginning of the San Bernardino Mountains. A smaller portion of the national forest extends west of the pass and borders the Angeles National Forest.

Two resort areas—Lake Arrowhead and Big Bear Lake—draw forest visitors for boating, swimming, and fishing in the summer, and downhill and cross-country skiing in the winter. Both are located northeast of the town of San Bernardino.

The resorts offer a luxurious contrast to the primitive gold-mining towns that once dotted the area. Visitors can tour the old mining sites by obtaining a self-guiding cassette tape from Fawnskin Ranger Station. Modern mining continues for limestone in nearby Holcomb Valley.

Primitive conditions are preserved in San Gorgonio Wilderness south of Big Bear Lake. The 59,000-acre wilderness surrounds San Gorgonio Peak. In the winter, hearty mountaineers hike to the peak to ski in two glacial bowls. Experienced skiers claim this is the best skiing in the entire forest—long, fast runs through virgin snow.

Less adventurous cross-country skiers find moderately challenging trails on former logging roads around the Barton Flats and Poopout Hill areas. In the summer, this area bustles with city children bused to one of twenty-one group camps built after the Depression. A popular half-mile nature hike for the blind at Whispering Pines

Bighorn sheep live high in the San Bernardino and San Gabriel mountains, but they are more often heard than seen as they deftly scramble up scree-covered slopes to escape the attention of humans. RON SANFORD

gives those with and without sight an opportunity to touch trees as they grow, die, and decay. Interpretive signs include explanations in Braille.

Eight easy to moderate trails follow creeks and lead to falls outside the San Gorgonio Wilderness. Equestrians gather at Heart Bar where a special horse camp is located.

One trail stands apart from the rest in length and legend. The Pacific Crest National Scenic Trail, a 2,620-mile route from Mexico to Canada, enters San Bernardino National Forest from the San Gabriel Mountains to the west and follows the San Bernardino Mountains to Nelson Ridge. There it turns south and heads past the San Gorgonio Wilderness to the San Jacinto Wilderness. In the southern block of the forest, the Pacific Crest Trail passes Tahquitz Peak, a landmark in local lore for centuries.

In parts of Southern California, think cactus when you think national forest. Although pine and cedar cover some high peaks, chaparral and succulents carpet much of the arid lowland. ROY MURPHY

Native American legend tells of an ancient chief named Tauquitch who grew greedy after years of benevolent leadership. Beautiful maidens began disappearing, and Tauquitch was caught and burned for his transgressions. But his soul sparked and drifted into the mountains. A brave warrior vowed to find and extinguish Tauquitch. Their furious battle carved the valleys and lakebeds and piled boulders on mountain sides. The warrior did not succeed, and the evil spirit supposedly lurks in the red rock that dominates the southern portion of San Jacinto Wilderness.

The wilderness lies in two sections surrounding Mt. San Jacinto State Park. Different hiking and camping rules apply in the state and federal lands, so check your maps. You'll need a free permit to enter the federal wilderness, and on summer weekends and holidays a quota limits the number of hikers who can use the Devil's Slide trail. Palm Springs Tramway rises more than six thousand feet from the nearby desert community to the state park, providing access to several trails that penetrate the national forest wilderness and continue to the town of Idyllwild.

As man encroaches on coyote range by building farther up the canyons of Southern California's national forests, the canines adapt. Reports of coyotes raiding pet food and eating small dogs and cats are common. JEFF FOOTT

Divided into three sections on the Santa Ana, Palomar, and Laguna mountain ranges, Cleveland National Forest stretches thirty-five miles from Orange County to within five miles of Mexico.

Cleveland differs from other national forests in several physical characteristics. Its mountains rise to peaks as low as three thousand feet and only as high as 6,140 feet at High Point, where the Palomar Observatory trains a 200-inch telescope on the heavens. Pines appear in the Laguna Mountain Recreation Area east of San Diego, and oaks grow in creek bottoms. But for the most part, Cleveland's steep slopes are covered with thickets of manzanita, ceanothus, and other chaparral brush. Still, Cleveland became a national forest for the same reason many of the state's wooded slopes became national forests—wildfire control and watershed protection.

Cleveland's fire-prone chaparral changes the nature of how visitors and foresters use the land. Campers are restricted to developed sites on the Santa Ana Mountains. You can roam the Palomar and Laguna ranges, but get a free permit first. Campfires and smoking are banned throughout the forest except in developed campgrounds. Only portable stoves can be used in wilderness camps, and free permits are required to enter all four wildernesses—Hauser, Pine Creek, Agua Tibia, and San Mateo Canyon.

The incendiary nature of the chaparral brush and the constant threat of strong winds called Santa Anas force foresters to be strict. The fierce winds can fan fires over ridges and fire breaks faster than fire fighters can stop them. So foresters prefer that visitors use developed campgrounds, trails, and sites like the Laguna Mountain Recreation Area.

Laguna Mountain Recreation Area has two campgrounds with 213 campsites, open year-round on a first-come, first-serve basis. Another eleven group camps with room for 625 people are available by reservation only. Yerba Santa is a four-site, wheelchair-accessible campground in the recreation area. In addition to the camps, two picnic grounds and seven hiking trails—including the southern-most portion of the Pacific Crest Trail on forest land—are located in the recreation area.

Autumn brings a touch of color to the oak-lined canyons and streambeds of Cleveland National Forest. ROY MURPHY

Day dawns over the Southern California desert and the Laguna Mountains in Cleveland National Forest, which stretches to within five miles of Mexico. DAVID MUENCH

The Palomar Mountains have six campgrounds—San Luis Rey, Crestline, Dry Creek, Dripping Springs, Oak Grove and Observatory. This area is mostly unroaded and surrounded by six Native American reservations and the Anza Borrego desert.

Three trails in the Agua Tibia Wilderness on the Palomar range climb into oak woodlands and small stands of Coulter pine and Douglas-fir. The trails, which range from about three miles to almost seven miles long, yield views of the observatory dome to the south and Mt. Baldy and the San Jacinto Mountains to the northeast.

Roads and people pass freely into and through the Santa Ana Mountains in the Cleveland National Forest. One of the busiest roads is California Scenic Highway 74, a commuter route between fast-growing Riverside and Orange counties. Forest rangers and sheriffs frequently untangle accidents that snarl traffic and upset drivers who try to double the speed limit of thirty-five miles per hour. The highway stretches east across thirty-five miles of desert floor to link the Cleveland and San Bernardino national forests.

Mountains and canyons in Cleveland National Forest are heavily settled from Modjeska Canyon to Aliso Canyon and Verdugo Potrero. Despite this intense human presence, mountain lions, deer, coyotes, and other wildlife still inhabit the area. To give nature a hand, foresters build "guzzlers"—small underground concrete pits that trap water for small animals and birds but protect them from predators while they drink.

In all, the Angeles, Cleveland, and San Bernardino national forests give Southern California aesthetic nourishment, wrap the rapidly expanding metropolitan area in an embrace of wildness, and provide the increasingly rare freedom of wide-open spaces. ■

THE FARTHEST VIEW OF ALL

From mountaintops in Angeles and Cleveland national forests, astronomers peer a billion light years (more or less) into space. Mt. Wilson Observatory in Angeles National Forest houses a 100-inch Hale telescope. Palomar Mountain Observatory in Cleveland National Forest contains a 200-inch Hale. From these stations atop 6,000-foot mountain peaks, astronomers have redefined the way we see the universe—and the way we travel around the earth and in space.

Both observatories have fabled pasts. Wilson's telescope mirror—refracted from French wine bottle glass—was hauled up treacherous Mt. Wilson on a bumpy jeep route in 1904. At the time, the clear Los Angeles Basin below and the surrounding pine and fir trees made Mt. Wilson an ideal spot for "good seeing." There were few city lights to interfere with starlight, and the trees stabilized the surrounding air, providing distortion-free viewing.

Astronomer Edwin Hubble in the 1920s and 1930s used the Mt. Wilson Observatory to discover that seeming wisps of gas were other galaxies. Hubble also discovered that galaxies were moving away from the sun, proving the universe was expanding.

Excessive light from the Los Angeles area forced the Carnegie Institution to close Mt. Wilson in 1984. Some privately funded research continues at the observatory, and a Pasadena-based group of astronomers announced plans in early 1989 to reopen the 100-inch telescope and use it to study the sun's 22-year magnetic cycle.

Astronomers at Palomar Mountain plan to work through the early 1990s remapping the stars. The 200-inch Hale at Palomar first mapped the northern hemisphere's skies in the 1950s, providing navigators and other astronomers with a guide to distant stars. The new map will provide more exact navigation information for sea and space travel by charting movements of stars over time.

Both observatories have visitor's galleries (but the telescopes are not open for public viewing) and are surrounded by national forest campgrounds.

Astronomers at Mt. Wilson Observatory in the Angeles National Forest and Palomar Observatory in the Cleveland National Forest have used 100- and 200-inch Hale telescopes, respectively, to observe solar phenomena and to map stellar constellations like the one seen below. JERRY SCHAD

ANGELES
NATIONAL FOREST DIRECTORY

POINTS OF INTEREST

CHILAO VISITOR CENTER on Angeles Crest Hwy. (2), about 27 miles north of La Canada-Flintridge. More than 20 indoor recreation, wildlife, and historical exhibits. Four outdoor nature trails, nearby campground and amphitheater with summer shows.

Mt. BADEN-POWELL north of Chilao on Angeles Crest Hwy., 9,399-foot peak that is home to 2,000-year-old limber pines.

EARTHQUAKE FAULT TOUR an 8-point self-guided auto tour starts at Big Pines on Angeles Crest Hwy., west of Wrightwood. Shows slipping and blocking along the San Andreas and San Jacinto fault zones.

RECREATION AREAS

BIG PINES Near Wrightwood on Angeles Crest Hwy., 12 campgrounds, four picnic areas, and nine trails are bunched in this area. Also close to two downhill ski slopes, nordic skiing at Jackson Lake, and the starting point for Earthquake Zone auto tour. Visitor center.

CRYSTAL LAKE 25 miles north of Azusa off Hwy. 39. Situated in oak and pine forests with a small lake and a visitor center.

WILDERNESS AREAS

CUCAGMONGA 8,581 acres divided between the Angeles and San Bernardino national forests, much of it above timber line on unstable, decomposing granite. Access from Icehouse Canyon trail above Mt. Baldy Village.

SAN GABRIEL 36,118 acres with five trails entering from Angeles Crest Hwy. and Hwy. 39 in the middle of the national forest, below Chilao. Rugged, wooded canyons with trout fishing along Bear Creek.

SHEEP MOUNTAIN 30,100 acres that contain 360 Nelson bighorn sheep. Five trails climb from Mt. Baldy Village and Big Pines to Mt. San Antonio, at 10,064.

RECREATIONAL ACTIVITIES

HIKING, RIDING, BICYCLING 623 miles of trails open to hikers, horseback riders, and mountain bicyclists. Trails range from short, self-guided nature trails to challenging high-elevation treks. 131 miles of Pacific Crest Trail down east side of Sierra Pelona Mtns., then east across San Gabriel Mtn. ridges and canyons.

CAMPING Forest is open to dispersed camping and Forest Service maintains 81 campgrounds. Fees charged vary, depending on water availability and toilet facilities.

PICNICKING Allowed throughout national forest, or at any of 33 designated spots.

ALPINE SKIING Six areas, most on Angeles Crest Hwy. between Chilao and Wrightwood, receive up to 60 inches of snow a year, some also make snow. Kratka Ridge (5 lifts), Mt. Waterman (3 lifts), Mt. Baldy (4 lifts), Mountain High East and Mountain High West (13 lifts), and Ski Sunrise (5 lifts).

CROSS-COUNTRY SKIING Trails follow national forest roads and are often groomed only by heavy use. Popular areas include East Blue Ridge, Table Mountain, and Grassy Hollow near Big Pines; Charlton Flats, Mt. Rooney Rd., Chilao Flats, Horse Flats, and Islip Saddle near Chilao Visitors Center.

SCENIC DRIVES Angeles Crest Hwy. is a candidate for national Scenic Byway status. It climbs quickly to pine and fir forests, and arches along the spine of the San Gabriel Mountains, yielding views of Los Angeles, the Pacific Ocean, and the high desert as well as waterfalls, campgrounds, and picnic grounds. Other scenic drives are the Old Ridge Route and Big Tujunga Canyon Rd.

HUNTING AND TARGET SHOOTING California Fish & Game license required. Hunting allowed throughout national forest high country except along all highways and inhabited areas. Target shooting allowed only in nine designated areas in the national forest—Middle, Kentucky, and Hunt areas off the Angeles Forest Hwy.; Rock and Pinyon areas off Little Rock Canyon Rd.; Tumbler off Rincon-Box Rd.; Pigeon off San Gabriel Canyon Rd.; and Ball and Horse areas off Big Pines Hwy.

FISHING California Fish & Game license required. Striped bass, catfish, rainbow and brown trout at Castaic Lake and Pyramid Lake. Exit I-5 at Castaic for Castaic Lake and Paradise Ranch for Pyramid. Fish & Game stocks rainbow in the east, west, and north forks of the San Gabriel River, Big Rock Creek, Little Rock Creek, Arroyo Seco, Big Tujunga Creek, and Bouquet Creek.

OFF-ROAD VEHICLES Green stickers and spark arrestors required. Three staging areas, 364 miles of designated ORV routes, 265 acres of open ORV areas. Rowher Flats has 31 miles of trails for intermediate to advanced riders, off Rush Canyon Rd. from Sierra Hwy. and Antelope (14) Hwy. Littlerock Reservoir has 125 acres of dry, flat, sandy and rocky land, take Hwy. 138 to Cheseboro Rd., then south 2.5 miles. San Gabriel Canyon has 150 acres of wet, rocky flats, crowded on weekends, entry fee charged. 12 miles north of national forest boundary on Hwy. 39.

ADMINISTRATIVE OFFICES

FOREST HEADQUARTERS 701 N. Santa Anita Ave., Arcadia CA 91006 (818) 574-1613

ARROYO SECO RANGER DISTRICT Oak Grove Park, Flintridge CA 91011 (818) 790-1151

MT. BALDY RANGER DISTRICT 110 N. Wabash Ave., Glendora CA 91740 (818) 335-1251

SAUGUS RANGER DISTRICT 30800 Bouquet Canyon Rd., Saugus CA 91350 (805) 296-9710

TUJUNGA RANGER DISTRICT 12371 N. Little Tujunga Canyon Rd., San Fernando CA 91342 (818) 899-1900

VALYERMO RANGER DISTRICT 34146 Longview Rd., Pearlblossom CA 93553 (805) 944-2187

SAN BERNARDINO
NATIONAL FOREST DIRECTORY

POINTS OF INTEREST

BIG BEAR LAKE and **LAKE ARROWHEAD** Resort towns on Hwy. 18 north of San Bernardino popular for skiing, fishing, swimming, and boating in the lakes.

TAHQUITZ PEAK and **SUICIDE ROCK** near Idyllwild, east of Riverside, best rock climbing in southern California.

PALM SPRINGS TRAM lifts riders from the desert to the mountains.

WILDERNESS AREAS

CUCAMONGA 8,581 acres of high country in Angeles and San Bernardino national forests. Much of area is at or above timberline.

SAN GORGONIO 59,000 acres including San Gorgonio Peak, 11,502 feet, the highest point in southern California. A mix of heavily wooded slopes, meadows, and barren peaks above timber line. Best wilderness skiing in southern California at Big Draw, Little Draw, and Christmas Tree Hill. Camp at 29 designated sites. Laced with easy, moderate, and difficult trails.

SAN JACINTO 20,500 acres of granite peaks, subalpine forests, and meadows. Quotas on 2.5-mile Devil's Slide Trail. Wilderness split into state and federal areas, with different restrictions in each. Summer camping is limited and divided into six zones.

SANTA ROSA 47,000 acres of rugged, remote country at the southernmost corner of the national forest. Wilderness permit not required.

RECREATIONAL ACTIVITIES

HIKING AND RIDING Almost 700 miles of trails, including 220 on the Pacific Crest Trail. All open to hikers, most to horseback riders and many non-wilderness trails open to mountain bicyclists. Horse camp at Heart Bar on Hwy. 38 above San Bernardino.

CAMPING Forest is open to dispersed camping, and Forest Service maintains 28 family campgrounds. Another 22 group camps are available by reservarion only.

PICNICKING Permitted throughout the national forest, or in 11 designated spots: Baylis and Switzer parks on the Arrowhead district; Aspen Glen and Meadow's Edge on the Big Bear district; Applewhite on the Cajon district; Falls, Jenks Lake, and Thurman Flats on the San Gorgonio district; Fuller Mill Crk., Lake Fulmor, and Lake Hemet on the San Jacinto district.

ALPINE SKIING Five developed resorts located near Arrowhead and Big Bear on Hwy. 18 above San Bernardino, the largest ski areas in southern California. Snow Valley (12 lifts), Gold Mine (8 lifts), Green Valley (4 lifts and tows), Snow Summit (9 lifts), and Snow Forest (5 lifts and tows).

CROSS-COUNTRY SKIING Ungroomed trails in the San Gorgonio Wilderness are popular; other trails near Poopout and Barton Flats on northern fringe of San Gorgonio Wilderness, at Lake Arrowhead and Big Bear Lake; at Snow Summit resort; and at Camp Whittle and Camp Lake Bluff.

SCENIC DRIVES San Bernardino national forest is most Sierra-like of all national forests in southern California. Hwys. 74 and 243 loop through heavily wooded, aromatic slopes in the San Jacinto section; Hwys. 18 and 38 ride the ridges of the San Bernardino Mountains and yield views of the hazy San Bernardino Valley to the south and west, and the desert to the east and north.

HUNTING AND TARGET SHOOTING Much of the national forest is designated as non-shooting area. Hunting allowed throughout national forest, except in designated non-shooting areas. California Fish & Game license required. Seasons on deer, bear, and a wide range of game animals and birds. Target shooting only at designated sites such as Lytle Creek, above Fontana. Other sites undergoing review.

FISHING Popular fisheries are Fuller Mill Creek, Dark Canyon Creek, and Strawberry Creek; the Santa Ana River and Jenks Lake on Hwy. 38 above San Bernardino; Holcomb Creek and Bear Creek west of Big Bear; Big Bear Lake and Lake Arrowhead; and Deep Creek-wild trout stream north of Lake Arrowhead.

OFF-ROAD VEHICLES AND SNOWMOBILES Green stickers and spark arrestors required. Designated trails on five ranger districts: Keller Peak Rd. and Strawberry Peak Rd. (Arrowhead Ranger District); Coxey Truck Trail, Holcomb Valley Rd., Polique Canyon Rd., Van Dussen Rd., and route 3N25 in Holcomb Valley (Big Bear); Stockton Flat Rd. (Cajon); Coon Creek Rd. (San Gorgonio); Black Mtn. Rd., Dark Canyon Rd., Idyllwild Control Rd., and Southridge Rd. (San Jacinto). Contact rangers for details.

ADMINISTRATIVE OFFICES

FOREST HEADQUARTERS 1824 Commercenter Circle, San Bernardino CA 92408 (714) 383-5588

ARROWHEAD RANGER DISTRICT P.O. Box 7, Rimforest CA 92378 (714) 337-2444

BIG BEAR RANGER DISTRICT P.O. Box 290, Fawnskin CA 92333 (714) 866-3437

CAJON RANGER DISTRICT Lytle Creek Ranger Station, Star Route, Box 100, Fontana CA 92335 (714) 887-2576

SAN GORGONIO RANGER DISTRICT Mill Creek Station, 34701 Mill Crk. Rd., Mentone CA 92359 (714) 794-1123

SAN JACINTO RANGER DISTRICT Idyllwild Ranger Station, P.O. Box 518, Idyllwild CA 92349 (714) 659-2117

CLEVELAND
NATIONAL FOREST DIRECTORY

POINTS OF INTEREST

PALOMAR OBSERVATORY is home to a 200-inch telescope now mapping the stars for the second time. Galleries open to visitors between 9 a.m. and 4:30 p.m. most days—telescopes not available for public viewing. Off Hwy. 6 atop Palomar Mtn.

RECREATION AREA

LAGUNA MOUNTAIN Two year-round campgrounds with 213 campsites, two picnic grounds, seven hiking and horseback riding trails. Volunteers lead nature walks and environmental talks on summer weekends at Laguna Lodge. Shooting, hunting, and off-road vehicles banned. On Sunrise Hwy. off I-8, east of El Cajon.

WILDERNESS AREAS

AGUA TIBIA 16,000 acres surrounded by Native American reservations and desert. Three trails into stands of Coulter pine, incense cedar and oak woodlands.

HAUSER AND PINE CREEK 21,000 acres on two adjacent areas, near the Mexican border, the southernmost wilderness areas in the U.S. Slopes climb from 2,000 to 4,000 feet. Creeks and streams generally dry through summer months.

SAN MATEO CANYON 39,500 acres, largest wilderness on the national forest.

Chaparral shrubs, with some oak, sycamore, and alder in stream beds and canyons.

RECREATIONAL ACTIVITIES

HIKING AND RIDING 331 miles of trails, including the southernmost portion of the Pacific Crest Trail between the Mexican border and the Anza-Borrego Desert. Many trails open to hikers and horseback riders, mountain bicycles not allowed. Trails generally course through rugged chaparral slopes; bring water.

CAMPING Limited to designated sites on the Trabuco district; open to dispersed camping on other districts. Fire permits required due to extreme, year-round fire hazards. Forest Service maintains 34 campgrounds.

PICNICKING Entire national forest open, or use picnic grounds in the Laguna Recreation Area; Lower San Juan and El Cariso off Hwy. 74 on the Trabuco district; or San Luis Rey at Lake Henshaw on Hwy. 79 and Inaja near Santa Isabel on Hwy. 78 on the Palomar district.

SCENIC DRIVES Ortega (74) Hwy. is a California Scenic Highway linking the Cleveland and San Bernardino national forests. In the Cleveland, the narrow, winding road climbs through chaparral and opens on small towns, meadows and hardwood stands. Use caution, the road is also a busy commuter route. Hwy. 6 from Oak Knoll to Palomar Mtn. climbs through Coulter pine and incense cedar on the way to the observatory.

HUNTING AND SHOOTING California Fish & Game license required. Seasons on upland birds and small animals. Check ranger districts for designated shooting areas.

OFF-ROAD VEHICLES Green stickers and spark arrestors required. Corral Canyon is a 1,800-acre area set aside for ORV cross-country touring. Off Corral Canyon Rd., 10 miles south of I-8. Wildomor ORV area is west of Lake Elisinore off I-15. ORVs also allowed to tour on dirt national forest roads such as Main Divide and Sitton Peak Rd. on Trabuco district.

ADMINISTRATIVE OFFICES

FOREST HEADQUARTERS 880 Front St., San Diego CA 92188 (619) 557-5050
DESCANSO RANGER DISTRICT 3348 Alpine Rd., Alpine CA 92001 (619) 445-6235
PALOMAR RANGER DISTRICT 1634 Black Canyon Rd., Ramona CA 92065 (619) 788-0250
TRABUCO RANGER DISTRICT 1147 E. Sixth St., Corona CA 91720 (714) 736-1811

Ventana Wilderness rises above scenic State Highway 1, which curves around the lip of the Santa Lucia Mountains on the Big Sur Coast in Los Padres National Forest. Kelp-lined coves provide sanctuary for sea otters, sea lions, and seals. LARRY ULRICH

Los Padres

N A T I O N A L   F O R E S T

Wilderness survives on the Central Coast

From Big Sur south to Santa Barbara lies a land of extreme contrast, Los Padres National Forest, the only California national forest with a coastline and beaches. Los Padres also has snow-covered peaks rising 8,000 feet above the sea, chaparral-covered hills, majestic coast redwoods, and rare Santa Lucia bristlecone firs. Endangered sea otters thrive in kelp beds along the national forest's coastline, and until recently, endangered California condors soared over the national forest's two condor sanctuaries.

Los Padres' climate provides more contrasts. Intense winter rains are sometimes followed by floods and landslides. In the summer, inland areas bake in arid, 110-degree days while fog dampens the coast. The hot, dry summers make Los Padres one of the most fire-prone national forests in California. Each year, wildfires burn an average of twenty thousand acres, and parts of the national forest must be closed during the fire season.

Floods and fires provided the impetus for establishing the Santa Barbara Forest Reserve—later to become the Los Padres National Forest—in 1891. By protecting and managing the area, local officials hoped to stop the flood-fire cycle and capture more water for surrounding towns and ranches.

To supply water, dam construction began on the Santa Ynez River in 1920, creating the Gibraltar Reservoir in the national forest above Santa Barbara. Today, three major reservoirs inundate the river within the national forest, and the national forest annually supplies 800,000 acre-feet of water for home, agricultural, and industrial use.

The reservoirs reduce the Santa Ynez River to a few pools in the summer months, but those pools provide a powerful attraction for Santa Barbara residents. Los Padres National Forest's Santa Ynez Recreation Area—a ten-mile continuous strip of beaches, picnic grounds, campgrounds, and parking lots—draws as many as 18,000 people on holiday weekends. Many come to escape cool summer fogs that blanket coastal areas while inland areas bask in warm sunshine.

Winter snow provides a different attraction, especially around 8,831-foot Mt. Pinos. As its name implies, Mt. Pinos is covered with an assortment of conifers, including Coulter, digger, and lodgepole pines. A volunteer nordic ski patrol grooms several trails for cross-country skiing.

Its various attractions make Los Padres one of the most popular national forests in the nation, ranking eleventh in overall visitation. Nonetheless, one-fourth of Los Padres' 1.7 million acres is undeveloped wilderness, and much of the rest is remote, rugged, and inaccessible.

That sounds like ideal habitat for the endangered California condor, which nested here for centuries. Unfortunately, increasing development in the huge bird's territory was enough to make it rare by 1900 and almost extinct by 1988. Los Padres National Forest contains two condor sanctuaries—both closed to human travel.

One development with a long history is the Sespe Oil

A DELUXE CONDORMINIUM WITH GREAT VIEW: NOT FOR SALE

Someday, perhaps as early as 1992, a California condor will again roost among the Topatopa Mountains in the 53,000-acre Sespe Condor Sanctuary in Los Padres National Forest.

If the graceful vulture's return comes that soon, it will be four years after a naturalist wrapped a protective shroud around the last wild Gymnogyps californianus. Only twenty-eight of the birds remain alive, all in captivity.

The birds soared out of prehistoric ages on nine-foot wingspans to range over California from the Fresno area to the Mexican border. By 1900, encroaching civilization conspired to make the carrion-eaters a rare species. The exact cause of their demise remains uncertain, although biologists suspect they were poisoned by eating lead pellets in game shot by hunters, suffered a reduced food supply as urbanization took over wild lands, and were shot by poachers and plinkers.

Scientists began anxious efforts to save the birds in 1976, when forty remained. Their last, desperate act was to capture all wild birds in hopes they could breed a new, stronger generation in captivity and train

those birds to avoid man-made pitfalls.

To that end, a condor-recovery team of biologists from the Los Angeles and San Diego zoos, the state Fish and Game Commission, and the U.S. Fish and Wildlife Service built a "condorminium" in the Sespe cliffs. The designer suite is a mesh-covered cave. The condors eventually will move from the cave to food platforms that will be built on stilts to foil bears and other predators.

After releasing the first of seventeen young Andean condors in late 1988 and

early 1989, scientists gradually reduced the amount of chopped rats and cow carrion left unobtrusively for the birds to consume. Team members will study the Andean birds, which are close cousins of the California condors, to see how well they adapt to the wild without an older generation to teach them the ways of the wild. When a full generation of captive-bred California condors is ready, the Andean birds will be recaptured, removed, and replaced by the California birds, if all goes well.

The California condor was once a common sight gliding above the state's valleys and foothills, but the last wild condor was captured at the Sespe Condor Sanctuary in 1988.

Field. Its discovery reads like a Hollywood script: Two boys from Pennsylvania come west after the gold rush and find their fortune in a thick black goo oozing out of the ground.

In 1884, Lyman Stewart and Wallace Hardison wandered into Tar Creek Canyon above Fillmore and found oil seeping into streams and out of hillsides. The mineral was so plentiful that at one point the company they formed (later Union Oil Co.) merely tunneled into a hillside and let the liquid run. Eventually, wells were drilled.

In the first one hundred years, the field produced twenty-seven million barrels of high-quality crude oil. The Sespe fields—the only working fields on a California national forest—produce about 600,000 barrels a year.

Elsewhere in Los Padres National Forest, increasing numbers of visitors seek quick, family-oriented hikes, tough motorcycle trails, challenging horse trails, and routes for mountain bicycles.

To minimize conflicts between different types of trail users, foresters designate separate trails. Off-road vehicles are restricted to specific areas, such as touring trails below Frazier Mountain west of the state ORV area at Hungry Valley, and La Panza east of Santa Maria. Mountain bikes are prohibited in wilderness areas but can use most other trails.

Mountain bicyclists skirt several wilderness areas on the Sierra Ridge Road—a fifty-mile route closed to all private vehicles except bicycles. The scenic road curves around the entire northern lip of the San Rafael Wilderness along the Sierra Madre ridge, then cuts between the San Rafael and Dick Smith wilderness areas before dropping into the Santa Ynez valley.

Halfway along Sierra Madre Ridge is Painted Rock Campground, one of the most accessible of several Native American rock art sites in the national forest. Many other Chumash nation sites are kept secret to limit vandalism.

Another scenic road—and one open to vehicles—lies closer to Santa Barbara. The Camino Cielo—"highway

---

Scrub oak, digger pine, and chaparral shrubs such as chamise and deer brush cover the low, dry San Rafael Mountains. Figueroa Mountain is a popular recreation area with picnic grounds, campgrounds, and trails into the San Rafael Wilderness.
DAVID MUENCH

of the sky''—serves a spectacular view of the Pacific Ocean on one side and several wilderness areas on the inland side as it travels along the Santa Ynez Ridge.

One of the wilderness areas is San Rafael, the nation's first official wilderness following the 1964 Wilderness Act. Within the wilderness, Hurricane Deck is a long, desolate, sandstone ridge lined with shale and carved into odd formations by howling winds. The deck lures many hikers and horseback riders. Two main trails, each with several spurs, leave from Nira campground at the foot of the wilderness. The Manzana Creek trail is soggy—bring extra boots—and historic. In about 10 miles it reaches the Manzana schoolhouse at an old homestead site. The Lost Valley trail climbs quickly and steadily to the top of Hurricane Deck.

Nira campground is located in the Figueroa Mountain Recreation Area. Three campgrounds, three picnic areas and twelve trails, including the four-mile Catway ORV route and the quarter-mile, wheelchair-accessible, self-guided Pino Alto nature trail, criss-cross the area.

The Mt. Pinos, Santa Ynez and Figueroa areas serve as a backdrop to the cities of Fillmore, Ventura, and Santa Barbara. Farther north along Highway 101, the Machesna Mountain and Santa Lucia wilderness areas climb behind Santa Maria and San Luis Obispo. These areas form a narrow band along the ridgetops of the La Panza and Santa Lucia ranges.

Still farther north along the Pacific Coast Highway—Highway 1—Big Sur Station serves as the major entry for 85 percent of the backpackers who climb into the rugged backcountry of Los Padres National Forest's Ventana Wilderness. Other entries are at Arroyo Seco

The red and yellow blooms of the red columbine nod in lowland spring breezes throughout California's national forests. The plant blossoms well into the summer in alpine meadows.
DAVID CAVAGNARO

and from Cone Peak above the southern Big Sur coast.

Nearly sixty rustic backcountry camps await hikers along 237 miles of trails in the Ventana Wilderness. One of the most popular destinations is the hot springs at Sykes camp about ten miles from the Big Sur Station. Throughout the wilderness, hikers pass numerous waterfalls, deep pools, and interesting geologic features such as faults and uplifts.

Steep ascents to meadows at five thousand feet within the Ventana Wilderness yield ocean views that seem limitless. Fogs seldom reach this elevation, but when fogs blanket the lower areas, the high country seems to float on a fluffy cushion of cotton—one more intriguing contrast within Los Padres National Forest. ∎

The Santa Ynez Valley stretches from Santa Barbara to the San Rafael and Dick Smith wildernesses. On summer weekends, the Santa Ynez River Recreation Area draws thousands of people hoping to trade damp coastal fog for 100-degree weather.
DAVID MUENCH

THE BEST OF BIG SUR

Los Padres National Forest contains one of California's best-known coastal areas—Big Sur—and one of the state's favorite scenic drives—Highway 1, the Pacific Coast Highway.

Between three million and four million tourists annually drive through the national forest on the Pacific Coast Highway. It is a breathtaking drive. Misty banks of fog rise off the pristine shore, the road hangs on the lip of cliffs and banks, and waterfalls tumble down high canyon walls. The narrow, curving road demands total attention, a difficult task when ocean and mountain vistas beckon.

Most of Los Padres National Forest's Big Sur coastal access is found on a twenty-mile stretch along Highway 1.

Four beaches and two campgrounds (all well-marked) attract surfers, jade hunters, hang-gliders, scuba divers, and touring bicyclists. Pfeiffer Beach, on the northern section of the Big Sur coast, is two miles off the highway on an unmarked road.

Rough tides shift Big Sur's beaches daily, even hourly in some places. Foresters find the Willow Creek beach rocky one day, sandy the next, and ladled with tide pools on the third.

As the ocean moves, so do its inhabitants. From Prewitt Ridge off the Nacimiento-Ferguson Road, whale watchers catch a glimpse of migrating California gray whales. The whales move south in November and December but often are too far offshore to see.

Come spring, cows herd their calves closer to shore and are easy to observe.

Sea otters, sea lions, and elephant seals thrive in the kelp beds beyond the surf line. Otters turned up here early this century after they were presumed extinct. Biologists found a colony of about fifty otters here in the 1930s. In the late 1980s, biologists started a controversial program of relocating part of the thriving colony to San Nicholas Island, seventy-five miles off the Southern California coast. The move was unpopular with commercial fisherman, who were concerned with the new competition, and with the otters, who immediately began swimming back to Big Sur.

GALEN ROWELL

LOS PADRES
NATIONAL FOREST DIRECTORY

P O I N T S   O F   I N T E R E S T

SESPE CONDOR SANCTUARY Former home of the last wild California condors and site of planned recovery effort.

SESPE OIL FIELD Only active oil field in a California national forest.

PACIFIC COAST HIGHWAY (State Hwy. 1) passes through and parallels Los Padres National Forest, the only California national forest with a coastline.

BIG SUR Beaches and campgrounds.

SALMON CREEK Southern-most stand of coast redwoods.

R E C R E A T I O N   A R E A S

ARROYO SECO Picnic area and three campgrounds especially designed to accomodate large families and groups. On the valley side of the forest due west of Greenfield on Monterey County Roads G16 and 3050. Area provides access to lakes and streams, and trailheads into Ventana Wilderness.

BIG SUR Two ocean-front camps with discounted areas for bicyclists and backpackers, four beaches, four picnic grounds. 16 rustic campgrounds in the bluffs and canyons above the coast. South of Monterey on Hwy. 1.

FIGUEROA MOUNTAIN Two campgrounds, three picnic areas, and a self-guided nature hike at Pino Alto. Vista point overlooking San Rafael Wilderness and Pacific Ocean, with explanatory signs, at Figueroa Mountain. One hour northeast of Santa Barbara on Hwy. 154 and Happy Canyon Rd.

SANTA YNEZ Seven campgrounds, four picnic areas, nature trails, and access to San Rafael Wilderness along 10-mile stretch of Santa Ynez River. Often full on summer days when ocean beaches cloaked in fog. Waterfalls, deep pools, remote hot springs. Forty minutes northeast of Santa Barbara on Hwy. 154 and the Paradise Rd.

MT. PINOS Access to ORV and snowmobile trails, popular cross-country skiing and snowplay area west of Frazier Park and I-5 on Frazier Park Road.

W I L D E R N E S S   A R E A S

VENTANA 164,178 acres above Big Sur coast. Trailheads at Big Sur, Arroyo Seco, and Cone Peak Road. Streams, waterfalls, and hot springs among steep canyons. Dense chaparral, with oak, madrone, and redwood in wet canyons. Camping limited to 54 designated sites along 237 miles of trails. Elevations from 600 to 5,862 feet.

SANTA LUCIA 21,678 acres on chaparral-covered Santa Lucia Mountains. Permanent stream in Lopez Canyon with a variety of streamside vegetation. Access by Lopez, Big Falls, Little Falls trails. Steep, rocky slopes home to rare Santa Lucia (bristlecone) fir. Elevations from 800 to 3,000 feet.

MACHESNA MOUNTAIN 20,000 acres on chaparral-covered La Panza Mountains. Access from hiking trails to north and west or from an off-road vehicle trail along north border. Elevations from 1,600 feet to 4,054-foot Machesna Mountain.

DICK SMITH 64,000 acres on rugged southern San Rafael Mountains. Steep, sparsely vegetated canyons; oaks and alders grow in high-elevation creeks that run year-round. Access to 49 miles of trail from Bluff Camp and Lower Alamar. Elevations between 3,750 and 6,541 feet.

SAN RAFAEL 149,170 acres on San Rafael Mountains. Closed by extreme fire hazard every summer and fall; 125 miles of trail open in winter and spring. Small Sisquoc Condor Sanctuary and trail around it closed to humans. Barren Hurricane Deck ridge and forested, 6,460-foot West Big Pine Mountain. Main access at Nira campground. Elevations 1,166 to 6,800 feet.

R E C R E A T I O N A L   A C T I V I T I E S

HIKING Most forest lands open. Foresters prefer hikers stay on designated trails, and much of the backcountry is closed in summer and fall by severe fire hazard.

CAMPING 75 campgrounds. Some have potable water and flush toilets, others are more primitive. Varying fees charged at campgrounds with water.

SKIING No downhill ski areas, but some groomed and non-groomed cross-country trails around Mt. Pinos.

PICNICKING Allowed anywhere in the forest. Designated sites in the Santa Ynez, Figueroa Mountain, Big Sur, and Arroyo Seco recreation areas.

SCENIC DRIVES California Hwy. 1 cuts along the edge of the North Coast Mountains and overlooks the Pacific Coast. California Hwy. 154 between Santa Barbara and Los Olivos yields spectacular views of the ocean, the Channel Islands, and the Dick Smith and San Rafael wilderness areas. Camino Cielo, above Santa Barbara, provides ocean and wilderness views.

MOUNTAIN BIKES Allowed on many trails except in wilderness areas. One popular trail follows jeep roads along the northern boundary of San Rafael Wilderness and between San Rafael and Dick Smith wilderness areas.

HUNTING AND FISHING California Fish and Game licenses required. All forest areas open except designated recreation areas. Seasons on mule deer, black bear, wild boar, wild turkeys, and band-tailed pigeons.

OFF-ROAD VEHICLES Green stickers and spark arrestors required. Restricted to designated trails near state Hungry Valley ORV area and La Panza.

A D M I N I S T R A T I V E   O F F I C E S

FOREST HEADQUARTERS 6144 Calle Real, Goleta, CA 93117 (805) 683-6711

MONTEREY RANGER DISTRICT 406 S. Mildred, King City, CA (408) 385-5434

MT. PINOS RANGER DISTRICT Frazier Park, CA 93225 (805) 245-3731

OJAI RANGER DISTRICT 1190 E. Ojai Ave., Ojai, CA 93023 (805) 646-4348

SANTA LUCIA RANGER DISTRICT 1616 N. Carlotti Dr., Santa Maria, CA 93454 (805) 925-9538

SANTA BARBARA RANGER DISTRICT Los Prietos, Star Route, Santa Barbara, CA 93105 (805) 967-3481

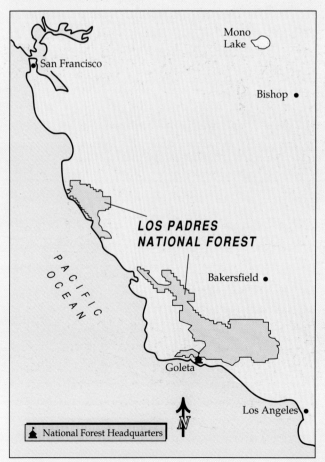

The hardy bark of the sequoia must protect the inner tree for as long as 3,000 years. The big tree needs moist, sandy soil and 45 to 60 inches of rain and snowmelt a year. It grows only in a 15-mile-wide band on the western slopes of the Sierra Nevada. JEFF FOOTT

Sequoia

Land of the giants

When turn-of-the-century loggers found giant sequoias in the southern Sierra Nevada, they thought they had discovered the ultimate timber tree. It took three decades of hard work and frustration to discover they were wrong.

By then, many of the majestic giants were gone. Fortunately, thirty-eight groves remained intact on the western slopes of Sequoia National Forest.

These giants form a large part of Sequoia National Forest's appeal. The national forest welcomes 2.4 million visitors a year, although not all come to see the big trees. Sequoia is chock-full of glacier-torn canyons, soaring granite monoliths, sparkling streams, and spectacular waterfalls.

Weather is another attraction. The western half of Sequoia boasts an almost Mediterranean climate like Southern California, with short, mild winters and long, dry summers. Along the Sierra peaks, snow falls from October to March in most years, providing water for alpine meadows filled with wildflowers. The eastern half of the national forest offers a contrast between arid plateaus and lush creek bottoms.

Nonetheless, when visitors choose between a trip to Sequoia National Forest, nearby Inyo and Sierra national forests, or Sequoia and Kings Canyon national parks, many people visit Sequoia National Forest because of the powerful pull of giant sequoias, cousins of the coast redwoods. Their magnetism has been at work since Yokut and Mono Indian tribes hunted here hundreds of years ago and left arrowheads scattered throughout the forest.

Loggers discovered giant sequoia in the late 1880s. Using

double-bladed axes, 12-foot cross-cut saws, springboards for elevated working platforms, and muscle and determination (and sometimes dynamite for particularly stubborn trees), the two- and three-man cutting teams, or choppers, attacked a single tree for days at a time. Gradually the choppers worked through the 10- to 30-foot-diameter trunk, bringing the giant crashing to earth.

During this time, promotion-minded businessmen chopped some of the larger trees to display before an awed public. One giant, the General Noble tree, was felled and hollowed out. Then its bark was cut into 14-foot sections and shipped to Chicago, where the 30-foot-wide trunk was reassembled to marvel visitors at the 1895 Columbian World Exposition.

Unfortunately for the loggers, many of the ancient trees—some 2,500 years old—shattered into large chunks when they hit the ground. Loggers left the broken wood where it fell and moved on to other trees. The amount of wasted wood—between 50 and 75 percent—staggered the profits of timber companies and forced them to abandon the trees.

Loggers didn't leave a moment too soon. Converse Basin in what later became Sequoia National Forest was nearly cleared of what had been the largest known grove of giant sequoias. Uncontrolled logging ended by 1935 when the Forest Service bought the basin and twenty thousand acres around Hume Lake.

The Hume Lake Ranger District lies fifteen miles north of the main body of the national forest, on the northern side of Sequoia National Park. The district contains fifteen sequoia groves. The twenty-foot-tall Chicago stump is here, and so is the Boole Tree, dubbed "King of the Big Trees" because it is the largest tree found in any national forest. Only two other trees—one in Sequoia National Park, the other in King's Canyon National Park—are larger. The Boole Tree, named for the forester who insisted it be spared from loggers, stands 269 feet tall and 112 feet around at its base.

To find these giants, follow California Highway 180 as it winds up the foothills, through grasslands and chaparral, until it takes you to a

Giant sequoias grow in about seventy groves on the western slopes of the Sierra Nevada. More than half the groves are in Sequoia National Forest. The big trees are named for their size—they are one of the largest species of trees on earth—and to honor Sequoya, a Cherokee chief who created an alphabet for his people.
DEDE GILMAN

conifer forest and the entrance to Sequoia National Park. Turn left and follow 180 north into Sequoia National Forest. In about five miles, you'll find spurs to the Chicago Stump and the Boole Tree.

Six miles beyond the Converse Basin, Highway 180 offers several access points into Sequoia National Forest's Monarch Wilderness. The highway itself provides a breathtaking sojourn through the steep canyon cut by the south fork of the Kings River.

Monarch Wilderness is crisscrossed with hiking and pack trails. Deer Cove trail gains three thousand feet in a little more than four miles. Three other trails climb toward 11,077-foot-tall Hogback Peak and then drop into Kings Canyon National Park. Nearby Jennie Lakes Wilderness is reached from three major trailheads.

The main body of Sequoia National Forest is accessible from three major roads on the west and south. Highway 190 follows the Tule River into the high country. Highway 155 is a half-hour tour through six different climates and vegetation zones. Highway 178 parallels the swift Kern River from Bakersfield to Isabella Reservoir, then continues east past the

The dense-growing trillium blooms in early spring, thriving in the shady understory of sequoia forests. Trilliums are also known as wake robins, referring to their early appearance in the spring.
JEFF FOOTT

From first thaw to first snow, the abundance of plants and wildflowers growing in high mountain meadows attracts backpackers, botanists, and photographers.   DEDE GILMAN

national forest to Highway 14.

The eastern half of the national forest is rimmed by 230,000 acres of three wilderness areas—Golden Trout, South Sierra, and Dome Land.

Golden Trout extends east into Inyo National Forest and is the largest and most diverse of the three wilderness areas. Its 147 miles of trails are served by eleven major trailheads.

Golden Trout Wilderness was formed to save the little kern golden trout in its evolutionary home. In addition, anglers must release their catches, dams are prohibited on the wild and scenic section of the Kern River and its tributaries, and riverbed spawning grounds are protected from excessive silt by the absence of road-building and logging.

Biologists from the Forest Service and the U.S. Fish and Wildlife Service are restoring the little kern's genetic purity by clearing out non-native fish such as rainbow and brook trout. These trout compete with the little kern and, in some cases, breed with it, creating hybrid trout. Chemicals and physical barriers have restored almost fifty miles of streams and four lakes for the exclusive use of the little kern.

Like Golden Trout Wilderness, South Sierra Wilderness extends east into Inyo National Forest. This wilderness is ideal for families with young children because the hikes are relatively easy, with plenty of large meadows and small streams for running, playing, and splashing.

Dome Land is a forgotten wilderness of craggy, barren peaks on the arid eastern side of the national forest. It is dominated by Pilot Knob—a white granite outcrop that shoots out of a sheath of crumbling red rock—and 8,363-foot Pine Mountain.

Visitors need not travel to the wilderness for adventure or scenery, however. Drivers make a full-day loop up Highway 190 to the Kern River, south along the Kern River Canyon road, and then west at Isabella on Highway 155. The route climbs through grasslands and moves quickly into mixed conifer stands.

Other scenic views include Dome Rock and the Needles. Spurs to these granitic monoliths are marked, and the formations are easily visible from Western Divide Highway. For a closer look, take the 2.5-mile hike—including 189 tortuous steps at the end—to Needles fire lookout. The reward is a spectacular, panoramic view—Mt. Whitney, the merging forks of the Kern River, earthquake-shattered Split Mountain,

THE BEAUTIFUL, DANGEROUS KERN RIVER

Three signs posted on the banks of the Kern River between Bakersfield and Isabella Reservoir are sobering reminders that for all their lovely scenery, national forests also contain hazards for the unwary and unprepared.

Bright red, four-inch-tall letters shout this warning at drivers entering the river canyon on Highway 178: "DANGER! DO NOT SWIM IN THE KERN RIVER. 144 LIVES LOST SINCE 1968." The count will surely have changed by the time you read this. Despite frequent patrols and repeated warnings by Sequoia National Forest officials, including annual messages on local television stations, the river kills about seven people a year.

The cold waters lure thousands of people on hot summer weekends and holidays. So many crowd the huge boulders along the banks that the area resembles a southern California beach. Inevitably, a few fail to heed the warnings.

"In some sections the river is deceptively calm. It looks dammed up, but it is traveling at the same speed as in the rapids—there just aren't any rocks there to make it look treacherous," says Jim Pearson, a Sequoia National Forest law enforcement agent. "A lot of drownings occur because when people jump in, they don't test the water. They don't look to see where the whitewater is, they don't listen to it, and they don't read the signs."

For all its wrath, the Kern does yield to recreation. With an average drop of thirty feet per mile, portions of the river

are outstanding white-water rafting and kayak runs. Be sure to get a permit (required from May 15 to September 15) and check with foresters for details on current conditions.

Each spring, melting snow brings a wash of green to Kern Canyon, right, but the rushing waters are a hazardous playground for city dwellers escaping the heat of Bakersfield and the urban clutter of Los Angeles.
ROB BADGER

and golden eagles playing on thermal air currents.

The Needles lure rock climbers as well. John Harlin's ''Climbers Guide to North America'' rates the ascents among the dozen best on the continent. They offer ''superb rock, tremendous views and unsurpassed crack and face climbing of all difficulties,'' yet are free of Yosemite crowds.

Highway 190 ending at Quaking Aspen takes you to the 22-mile Summit National Recreation Trail. The trail, one of a dozen in the Tule River high country, is open to motorcycles, hikers, and horses. A nearby grove of giant sequoia is best experienced by taking the quarter-mile, self-guided Trail of 100 Giants across Western Divide Highway from Redwood Meadow campground.

The last leg of the loop—from Isabella over Greenhorn Summit on Highway 155 to Glennville—is a short course in forest diversity. In mid-November, golfers play in their shirt sleeves on barren links at the north end of Isabella Reservoir. At Greenhorn, a seven-mile, 13-percent grade climbs from the lake to elevations where snow lies on the ground and cedars scent the air. Alders and oak line Cedar Creek, while the drive to Glennville goes through manzanita and grasslands.

Visitors may want to interrupt their drive with a stop at one of several small resorts that offer a good cup of coffee, a warm bed near a trailhead, and cross-country ski rentals and lessons—all part of Sequoia National Forest's appealing diversity. ■

GIANTS OF THE EARTH

Like their dinosaur contemporaries, giant sequoias flourished across much of North America some sixty million years ago. Unlike the giant reptiles, however, Sequoiadendron giganteum *survived all the changes that followed, including Ice Age glaciers that flowed into California about three million years ago.*

Tough and resilient, sequoias endure hardships that kill other trees. Their tan-colored bark is one- to two-feet thick and protects them from insects and infernos, although some trees are peppered with charred areas and pocked with 10-, 15-, and 20-foot scars at their bases.

These giants are found in seventy groves in a 260-mile belt spanning elevations between 3,000 and 8,900 feet along the western slopes of the Sierra Nevada, stretching from Foresthill Divide in Tahoe National Forest to Deer Creek in Sequoia National Forest. A cousin, Sequoia sempervirens *or coast redwood, grows along the misty California coast from the Oregon border south to Salmon Creek in the Los Padres National Forest.*

Coast redwoods grow taller than the inland sequoias, which are squatter and live longer, but both are majestic monarchs that link present generations with ancient history. While they are not the oldest living things on earth—ancient bristlecone pines in California's Inyo National Forest take that honor—some of the giants in Sequoia National Forest are 3,500 to 4,000 years old.

The big trees have fascinated people throughout history. Piute and Shoshone Indians drank sequoia sap to tap its majestic power. Conservationist John Muir called them "the greatest of living things." The trees were named to honor Cherokee Indian chief Sequoya, who invented a Native American alphabet.

For all their huge size, the trees have humble beginnings. The egg-shaped cones, which take two years to mature, are rarely more than one to three inches long, and they nurture incredibly tiny seeds—half a dozen can fit on a dime.

Under the right conditions, foresters allow prescribed fires in sequoia groves to burn away built-up piles of needles and fallen branches to provide cleared areas for future seedlings. The sequoia's tan bark is one- to two-feet thick and often pocked with black centuries-old fire scars.
GERRY REYNOLDS

SEQUOIA
NATIONAL FOREST DIRECTORY

P O I N T S   O F   I N T E R E S T

GIANT SEQUOIA 38 groves scattered throughout the national forest. 15 groves in the Hume Lake Ranger District, including Chicago Stump and Boole Tree, off Hwy. 180, east of Fresno.

WILD AND SCENIC RIVERS North Fork Kern, South Fork Kern, Kings, and South Fork Kings.

THE NEEDLES 10 granite spires, rock climbing, a fire lookout atop one spire. Off Western Divide Hwy. near Quaking Aspen, two mile hike from end of road.

R E C R E A T I O N   A R E A S

KERN PLATEAU Four campgrounds, public pastures for boarding horses, trailheads to Dome Land, Golden Trout, and South Sierra wildernesses, off-road vehicle trails, and miles of streams and rivers for fishing and rafting. Check with Cannell Meadow ranger district for fee information.

KINGS RIVER SPECIAL MANAGEMENT AREA Three free campgrounds, Kings River National Recreation Trail and other trails, Boole Tree, and Garlic Falls. White-water rafting and kayaking on the Kings River, between Garnet Dike and Kirch Flat.

W I L D E R N E S S   A R E A S

DOME LAND 95,000 acres marked by granite domes in high elevations and bisected by South Fork Kern River, the southernmost golden trout fishery in California. Pinyon pine and firs in canyons; 45 miles of trails.

GOLDEN TROUT 306,000 acres of lush meadows and vast pine and fir forests, partly on Inyo National Forest. Kern River is home to golden trout and the threatened little kern golden trout.

JENNIE LAKES 10,500 acres of red fir, lodgepole pine, and meadows dashed with wildflowers in the spring. Two trails enter the area and lead to adjacent Kings Canyon National Park.

MONARCH 24,000 acres from 2,000 feet to 11,000 feet. Steep canyons and a range of plants from desert yucca to giant sequoia. Seven trails, some that lead into Kings Canyon National Park.

SOUTH SIERRA 63,000 acres of rolling meadows on the Sequoia side, steep and craggy on the Inyo National Forest side. 30 miles of trails, including portions of the Pacific Crest Trail.

R E C R E A T I O N A L   A C T I V I T I E S

HIKING AND RIDING Almost 830 miles of trails—including 49 miles of Pacific Crest Trail in three sections—open to hikers, horseback riders, and mountain bicyclists.

CAMPING Allowed throughout the national forest, or at any of 50 campgrounds maintained by the Forest Service. Check with district rangers for fee and reservation information.

PICNICKING Allowed throughout the national forest, or at 12 designated day-use sites near lakes and streamside campgrounds.

ALPINE SKIING Shirley Meadows (3 lifts and rope tows) off Hwy. 155 just south of Greenhorn.

CROSS-COUNTRY SKIING On most national forest backcountry roads and trails, such as Quaking Aspen trail. Marked trails at Peppermint, on Hwy. 190 near the Needles; Cherry Gap, Quail, and Big Meadows on the Hume Lake district; Greenhorn Summit on Hwy. 155; Kern Plateau.

WHITE-WATER RAFTING AND KAYAKING Runs rated from Class III (moderate) to Class VI (expert) on lower and upper Kern River and its forks.

SCENIC DRIVES Hwy. 190 loops east and south from Porterville, climbing through fir, pine, and giant sequoia stands to a ridgeline called western divide. Highway ends at Quaking Aspen, but follow county road SM99 east to Johnsondale, then south to Kernville and Lake Isabella. Hwy. 155 is a quick trip in botany: the road starts in lowland chaparral, then climbs into pine, fir, and cedar stands at Greenhorn Summit, before dropping to arid Lake Isabella. From that reservoir, Hwy. 178 winds southwest out of the national forest along the treacherous Kern River and its rocky canyon.

HUNTING California Fish & Game license required. Seasons on mule deer, black bear, valley quail, squirrel, and band-tailed pigeon.

FISHING California Fish & Game license required. Almost 1,300 miles of streams and rivers and 180 acres of lakes, many stocked with rainbow trout.

OFF-ROAD VEHICLES AND SNOWMOBILES Green stickers and spark arrestors required. Almost 1,000 miles of national forest roads and 320 miles of designated trails. Much ORV use centered on Kern Plateau. Snowmobile areas at Peppermint and Quaking Aspen on Hwy. 190, Big Meadows, and Hume Lake.

A D M I N I S T R A T I V E   O F F I C E S

FOREST HEADQUARTERS 900 W. Grand Ave., Porterville CA 93257 (209) 784-1500

CANNELL MEADOW RANGER DISTRICT P.O. Box 6, Kernville CA 93238 (619) 376-3781

GREENHORN RANGER DISTRICT 800 Truxten Ave., Room 322, Bakersfield CA 93301 (805) 861-4212

HOT SPRINGS RANGER DISTRICT Route 4, Box 548, California Hot Springs CA 93207 (805) 548-6503

HUME LAKE RANGER DISTRICT 35860 E. Kings Canyon Rd., Dunlap CA 93261 (209) 338-2251

TULE RIVER RANGER DISTRICT 32588 Highway 190, Springville CA 93265 (209) 539-2607

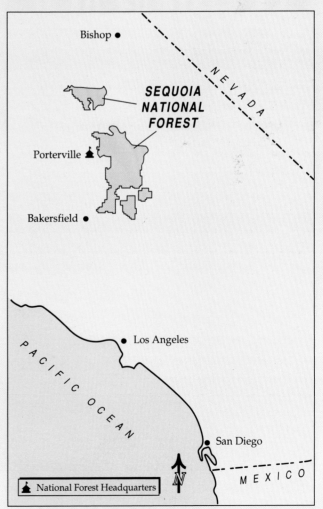

A harvest moon and lingering alpenglow bathe Mt. Whitney's sheer scarp in an eerie pink glow.
The climb to Whitney's summit is so popular that a quota limits overnight hikers. PAT O'HARA

Inyo and Toiyabe

*The oldest,
the highest,
and the
wildest*

Inyo and Toiyabe national forests straddle the California-Nevada border for 150 miles from Lake Tahoe south to the border town of Oasis. Toiyabe covers the northern section, Inyo the southern, and both take your breath away for dazzling beauty and diversity.

These national forests share certain characteristics, but they also differ in several ways, including their administration. Most of the Inyo National Forest lies in California, but some spills into Nevada. Most of Toiyabe lies in Nevada, but part of it laps into California. Inyo joins seventeen other national forests in California in the Forest Service's Pacific Southwest Region. Toiyabe is part of the Forest Service's Intermountain Region that covers Nevada, Utah, and parts of Idaho and Wyoming.

Of course, mountains, streams, and wild animals know no political boundaries, and Inyo and Toiyabe national forests contain all of these outdoor attributes and more. From the tallest mountains in California to the oldest living things on earth, from a strange lake to tumbling streams, from thick woods to arid slopes, Inyo and Toiyabe national forests present an outstanding array of natural wonders.

INYO

N A T I O N A L   F O R E S T

The longest national forest in California, Inyo National Forest stretches 165 miles along U.S. Highway 395 from Mono Lake to Owens Lake. Another long section marches down the California-Nevada border before turning south to parallel Owens Valley.

To the west of Owens Valley, Inyo National Forest rises with the jagged peaks of the Sierra Nevada. To the east, Inyo contains the White Mountains and the edge of the Great Basin desert. The mountains are climatic war zones, the high ground in a never-ending battle between lushness and desert. But unlike most battles, this one produces a land of spectacular and diverse sights.

Near the southern end of Inyo's 1.9 million acres, Mt. Whitney rises 14,495 feet above sea level to the highest point in the forty-eight contiguous states. Sixty-five miles north and east, the Ancient Bristlecone Pine Forest shelters a wizened, gnarled, 4,700-year-old tree, the oldest living thing on earth. Almost due west of the ancients, Mammoth Mountain attracts four million skiers each year. And at the national forest's northern edge lies Mono Lake, a first-ever national forest scenic area.

Inyo's weather adds to the diversity. Sudden snowstorms blow in a blizzard any day of the year along much of the Sierra crest. Lenticular clouds that look like willowy chef's hats spun on a potter's wheel signal a weather change when they hang above the peaks. Hot temperatures prevail in the southern portions of the national forest, and in the northern sections, temperatures climb over 100 degrees in the summer and plummet below zero in the winter.

Highway 395 links Inyo National Forest to the urban world. Most visitors make the four-hour drive north from Los Angeles, although some drive two hours south from Reno. Roads branching off the highway lead into steep canyons, hot springs, 1,200 miles of trails, 2,200 campsites and 13 backcountry pack stations.

Perhaps seventy percent of Inyo National Forest's ten million tourists visit the Sierra Nevada side of the forest, where hundreds of rugged peaks form the skylines of five designated wilderness areas—South Sierra, Golden Trout, John Muir, Ansel Adams, and Hoover.

South Sierra Wilderness is dominated by 9,884-foot Round Mountain and 12,123-foot Olancha Peak, the most southern of the great Sierra peaks. The Pacific Crest Trail stitches through a portion of the wilderness before continuing into Golden Trout Wilderness.

Golden Trout Wilderness, which like the South Sierra Wilderness spreads west into Sequoia National Forest, protects creeks and streams that feed the Kern River

THE ANCIENT ONES

In the White Mountains of Inyo National Forest, ancient bristlecone pine, (Pinus longaeva) lift twisted, threadbare branches from short, stout trunks in solemn gestures that seem to accept the travail of long life.

Before Jesus Christ was born, before Alexander the Great conquered Egypt in 332 B.C., seventeen bristlecone pines now standing on the White Mountains were already two thousand years old. The environment for these venerable trees is no lush, protected Eden. Rather, the eastern slopes of the Whites are a steep, dry, wind-blown Hades that would seem to destroy whatever dared dig roots here.

The pale dolomite soils hold little water but they sustain the bristlecone. Approaching Schulman Grove, the ground beneath the stand appears white-washed and few trees cross the border where the limestone ends. The rare trees only grow between 10,000 and 11,000 feet, a zone where harsh winds whip over the top of the Sierra thirty miles west and tear through to the Great Basin desert on the east. Very little precipitation makes it over the Sierra, and most of what does takes the form of driving snow.

Bristlecones survive by going slow. In drought years, the trees might not grow at all. In good years, they might add an inch. Some older trees are stripped of all but a few inches of bark by wind-driven sand and grit. Those inches carry life to the wee tips of the tree, where tiny, soft needles live for thirty years before falling away. The slow growth makes tight-grained, resinous wood that cabinetmakers covet, and many bristlecones were harvested until the Forest Service protected what are now the Schulman and Patriarch groves, part of the Ancient Bristlecone Pine Forest Botanical Area.

The trees have a higher and better use than cabinetry. Through the science of dendrochronology—studying the history of climatic and environmental changes by analyzing tree rings—archaeologists have refined carbon-dating. Scientists study pencil-thin borings pulled from living and dead trees to establish historic data. The tree ring patterns are so precise that scientists can trace events as far back as 3675 B.C.

The bristlecone groves are found east of Big Pine off Highway 168. There are two self-guided hikes at the Schulman Grove, which was named to honor Edmund Schulman, a University of Arizona scientist who discovered the oldest living tree. Visitors pass the 4,700-year-old tree on the four-mile Methuselah Walk, but it is not identified so vandals and souvenir hunters will not harm it. The Patriarch Grove is another twelve miles above Schulman Grove on White Mountain Road. Campgrounds, picnic areas, and vista spots—including the spectacular Sierra View—await visitors.

Two bristlecone pines twist in the howling winds at 11,000 feet on the Inyo National Forest's White Mountain. LARRY ULRICH

and nurture the little kern golden trout, a threatened species. The wilderness boundary closes to within a half-mile of Highway 395 between Olancha and Big Pine, and its northwest corner forms a border with Sequoia National Park. Most trails follow steep canyons into and through the wilderness.

The southernmost of Inyo National Forest's 519 glacial lakes appear near the border between the Golden Trout and John Muir wilderness areas. The lakes lie in the shadows of nine peaks that rise above 13,000 feet, including four above 14,000 feet. From Mt. Langley to Mt. Whitney to Tunnabora

Peak, these summits form the spectacular southern flank of an army of sheer granite spires exceeding 13,000 feet.

A 10.7-mile trail leads to the 14,495-foot summit of Mt. Whitney. The trail starts at 8,365 feet at the Whitney Portal west of Lone Pine. The hike is strenuous, especially for those not acclimated to high elevations. The best way to become acclimated is to camp at one of three Whitney Portal campgrounds. Contact the Forest Service's Lone Pine office for information and wilderness permits

The John Muir Wilderness in Inyo National Forest

One of a half-dozen species of evening primrose found in California, rock fringe, right, blooms red, rose, and pink all summer in High Sierra passes. LARRY ULRICH

Tioga Lake, far right, a glacial cirque nestled between Tioga and Gaylor peaks, lies within a mile of Yosemite National Park and about 10 miles west of Mono Lake. Trails into the Ansel Adams and Hoover wilderness areas begin at a small, primitive campground at lakeside. ED COOPER

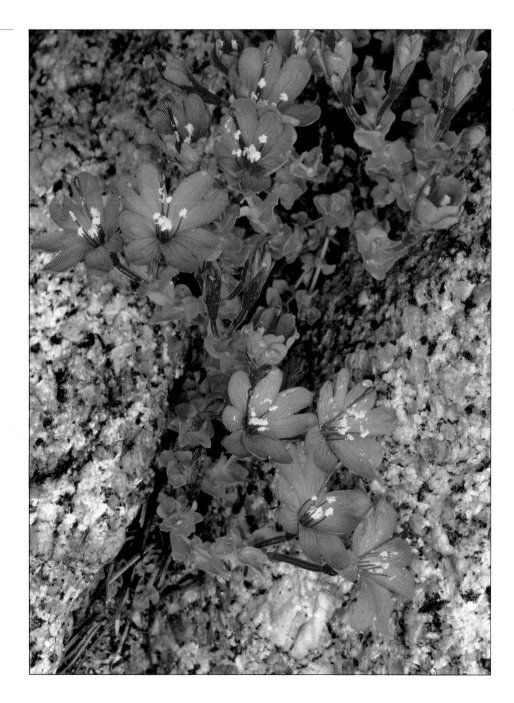

snakes north for seventy-five miles in a thin sliver squeezed between Highway 395 and the Sequoia and Kings Canyon national parks. North of Whitney, the wilderness loops around the top of Kings Canyon and into the Sierra National Forest until it abuts the Ansel Adams Wilderness just east of Mammoth Lakes and the Devil's Postpile National Monument.

Along the way, the John Muir Wilderness encompasses the 22,000-acre California Bighorn Sheep Zoological Area. Under an agreement with Inyo National Forest, the California Department of Fish and Game manages the area, which is divided into sections around Mt. Baxter and Mt. Williamson. About thirty sheep thrive in the Williamson portion and 175 live in the rugged country around Baxter. Baxter herd progeny have been reintroduced throughout the Sierra high country. Bighorn hunting is banned in the area, and trails are few, but good trout fishing exists deep in the zoological area.

Twenty-seven major trails enter the John Muir wilderness from the east. To limit environmental damage and provide more solitude to backcountry trekkers, wilderness permits are required. Most paths travel along canyons and creeks. None, not even the Pacific Crest Trail, follow the rugged Sierra ridge.

Throughout the area, wildlflowers blossom in hundreds of alpine meadows. Lupine, shooting star, and wooly mule ear blaze lavender and yellow, while Indian paintbrush glow red and orange.

The long, scenic drainage of Rock Creek lures hikers in the summer and cross-country skiers in the winter. Many tour the area by "hut-hopping," or traveling from one backcountry hut to another. The huts are operated by resorts located west of Highway 395 above Tom's Place. The area's nordic skiing ranks among the best in the West.

Downhill skiers by the millions travel another twenty miles north to Mammoth Lakes and June Lake, where miles of ski slopes wind through national forest land.

In the summer, Mammoth draws about two million tourists who hike, sight-see, or compete in a growing list of athletic endeavors such as mountain bike races and triathlons. A few come to see or bathe in the roiling waters of Hot Creek, a few miles south of the mountain, east of Highway 395.

Many Mammoth visitors take a scenic drive, including a shuttle bus that travels eight miles to Devils Postpile National Monument. Dozens of short, self-guided hikes within the national forest educate and entertain visitors.

Farther north, the rugged high country of Ansel Adams Wilderness crosses the Sierra crest into Sierra National Forest. Like the John Muir, the Ansel Adams Wilderness was named to honor a man who helped create a national awareness of wilderness values. Muir did it with his writing. Adams used exquisite black-and-white photographs that etched the severe, pristine landscape in our memories forever.

Thousand Island Lake is one of the most visited—and most photographed—backcountry destinations in the Ansel Adams Wilderness, which is why a trip there requires a wilderness permit. The Pacific Crest Trail skirts the north shore of Thousand Island on a four-mile stretch through the wilderness from Devil's Postpile to Donohue Pass and Yosemite.

Hikers climb through stands of red fir, Jeffrey and lodgepole pine, mountain hemlock, and quaking aspen trees—rising rapidly from 7,600 to above 10,000 feet.

A hiker atop 14,495-foot Mt. Whitney, left, leaps higher than the highest point in the forty-eight contiguous states. California's tallest peak is one of the main attractions in Inyo National Forest. GALEN ROWELL

A few hundred mountain lions, right, still roam the High Sierra, feeding on mule deer, bighorn sheep and jackrabbits. Shy creatures, they rarely allow themselves to be caught on camera. JEFF FOOTT

Then the trails level into alpine meadows and barren granite floors backed by the stark, volcanic Minarets Range with ten peaks rising above 13,000 feet.

While Inyo's Sierra Nevada section receives the most visitation, the White and Inyo mountains rise to the east on the border of the Great Basin. Although the valleys that separate the Sierra from the Whites are only ten miles wide in some places, they form a gulf between two vastly different worlds. The White Mountains are barren and dry, marked by stark white dolomite soils and twisted, ancient bristlecone pines.

These mountains form a single massive block 110 miles long. Average elevations are around 10,000 feet, with a dozen peaks in the White Mountains rising well above 11,000 feet and half that many in the Inyos. At 14,242 feet, White Mountain Peak is the third-highest in California and the highest outside of the Sierra. Nevada's highest point, 13,143-foot Boundary Peak, rises near the state line in Inyo National Forest.

To the north, the White Mountains sink into Mono Basin, home to limestone pinnacles—tufa towers—in Mono Lake, the first national forest scenic area and another incredible sight within Inyo National Forest.

The rolling cauldrons of Hot Creek, left, east of Mammoth Lakes, spew sulfurous steam, scalding water—and sometimes cyanide—from the bowels of a still-active volcano. JOHN DITTLI

Resort operators at Mammoth Lakes create nordic ski trails around their popular downhill slopes, top right. Hundreds of miles of ungroomed wilderness trails throughout California national forests are open to experienced cross-country skiers. FRANK S. BALTHIS

Snowmobiling is a popular High Sierra sport, bottom right, with designated routes and areas apart from wildernesses and nordic ski-touring areas. JOHN DITTLI

Glacier-covered Mt. Ritter, at 13,157 feet, and Banner Peak, at 12,945 feet, tower over Ediza Lake in the Ansel Adams Wilderness, far right. ED COOPER

MAGIC WATERS OF MONO LAKE

Mono Lake's magic waters have captivated writers such as John Muir and Mark Twain and industrialists such as William Mulholland. In 1897 Twain marveled at the cleansing powers of the apparently dead sea. A year earlier, Muir gaped at the pristine lake planted between a desert and volcanoes. Mulholland viewed Mono in the 1930s as a potential water supply for Los Angeles after nearby Owens Lake was drained dry.

A series of legal rulings and the Forest Service's management plan for the Mono Basin Scenic Area promise to protect Mono Lake from being drained. Courts and foresters recognize that Mono's salt waters and mysterious lunar landscape are fragile and unique. Five freshwater streams feed the lake, but there is no natural outlet. As water evaporates, it leaves minerals behind. The lake is three times as saline as the Pacific Ocean.

The lake forms critical habitat for millions of birds. On their migratory journeys across the Great Basin desert, nearly one million eared grebes and 150,000 phalaropes stop at Mono Lake to feast on brine shrimp and flies. Each bird may eat thousands of shrimp every day, doubling its weight before resuming its migration. About twenty-five percent of the North American population of California gulls nests on Negit Island.

All around the shoreline, majestic yet fragile tufa towers stand like centurions guarding an ancient lifeline. The towers form when calcium-rich spring water bubbles up through the carbonite-loaded lake water. The minerals combine and settle, forming the towers.

Like the brine shrimp-fly-fowl ecosystem, the tufa towers are threatened by declining lake levels. Starting in 1941, Los Angeles diverted enough water from four of the seven streams that feed Mono to drop the lake's level by more than forty feet. That threatened the food chain, exposed the

Mystic tufa towers that form underwater when calcite and sodium mix and settle rise like sentinels on the shores of ancient Mono Lake. The towers stop growing when exposed to air. Their shoreline presence is testimony to falling lake levels caused by diversion of Mono's tributaries to slake Los Angeles' thirst. GALEN ROWELL

gulls to predators, and left the pristine towers vulnerable to inquisitive tourists who destroyed the tufa by climbing on it and chipping away a souvenir.

The Mono Lake Committee, a grassroots group some ten thousand strong, began fighting Los Angeles in 1978 and scored early victories when judges ruled the powerful southern California city was required to release enough of the diverted stream water to maintain life in the streams. The Forest Service took control of almost 74,000 acres around the lake when Congress created the first national forest scenic area in 1984.

TOIYABE

Toiyabe National Forest's 3.5 million acres make it the largest national forest in the lower 48 states. Most of Toiyabe lies in Nevada, but its California sections are natural jewels. From Mono Lake north to Lake Tahoe, Toiyabe crosses the Nevada border to form the eastern boundary of four California national forests—Inyo, Stanislaus, Eldorado, and Tahoe.

The Hoover Wilderness reaches into Toiyabe National Forest from Inyo National Forest five miles west of Mono Lake. The wilderness is peppered with glacial lakes, many with good fishing for rainbow and brook trout. Trails lead to most lakes, and some trails continue into Yosemite National Park.

Many of Toiyabe's lakes and streams are good trout haunts, although Silver King Creek in Fishlake Valley is off limits since it is the only remaining home for the endangered Piute cutthroat trout. The national forest is also black bear country, as is much of the Sierra Nevada. Hikers hang food from tree limbs twenty feet off the ground to avoid close encounters. Other wilderness animals include mule deer, bobcats, coyotes, and mountain lions.

Drivers on California Highway 108 and hikers on the Pacific Crest Trail switch from alpine meadows to desert in less than a mile as they cross the Sonora Pass between the Stanislaus and Toiyabe national forests. The summit vista offers quaking aspen in the Stanislaus meadows and miles of barren, blue Excelsior Mountains in the Toiyabe and the Great Basin desert beyond.

Farther north near Lake Tahoe, the Carson District of Toiyabe National Forest contains 10,000-foot peaks, deep canyons, high meadows, clear streams, and roaring waterfalls.

Summer temperatures in Toiyabe National Forest range from the 70s to below freezing. The High Sierra passes often do not open until June or July and close again with heavy snows that start in November.

The Toiyabe and its neighboring California national forests contain several historic mining areas. A gold rush swept Dogtown and Monoville in 1859 and later boom towns such as Bodie, Aurora, and Lundy sprang up around silver and gold mines. The ghost town of Bodie attracts tourists eager to taste the essence of the wild west in its mining days. ∎

Campgrounds, right, in California's national forests vary from primitive sites without water or toilets to developed areas with picnic tables and running water.
TOM MYERS

Wild irises wave in Leavitt Meadows, far right, in the Toiyabe National Forest. Toiyabe, most of which is in Nevada, crosses into California and forms the eastern border of four of the state's national forests—Inyo, Eldorado, Stanislaus, and Tahoe. JEFF GNASS

Mountain primroses bloom in alpine meadows and passes throughout the summer. DAVID CAVAGNARO

INYO
NATIONAL FOREST DIRECTORY

POINTS OF INTEREST

MONO LAKE supports millions of migratory and nesting birds, and the lake's unique chemistry leads to the formation of mysterious tufa towers. The one-million-year-old lake is on Hwy. 395, at Lee Vining.

HOT CREEK GEOTHERMAL AREA is a series of roiling hot springs, steam vents, and sinkholes that testify to volcanic activity perhaps 1,000 feet below.

ANCIENT BRISTLECONE PINE FOREST in the White Mountains east of Bishop is home to the oldest living beings on the earth—including a 4,700-year-old bristlecone pine.

MT. WHITNEY at 14,495 feet is the highest peak in California and the second highest peak in the U.S. Whitney summit trail permits are required. Contact district ranger for fee, quota, and reservation information.

RECREATION AREA

MAMMOTH LAKES Mammoth Mountain and nearby June Lake are year-round draws. Winter brings nearly four million skiers; fewer come in spring, summer, and fall to see wildflowers, picnic, boat, or compete in mountain bicycle races and triathlons. Mandatory shuttle bus makes 11 stops between town and Devil's Postpile National Monument—at 7 campgrounds, 2 picnic grounds, Minaret Vista, and Mammoth Mtn. ski resort. Check at Mammoth ranger station for schedule and fare information.

WILDERNESS AREAS

ANSEL ADAMS 228,500 acres partly in Sierra National Forest. Elevations to 13,000 feet. Red fir stands at lower elevations give way to alpine meadows and barren, granite moraines at higher levels. Hundreds of streams and lakes; Minarets Range offers challenging ascents for experienced rock climbers

GOLDEN TROUT 305,000 acres partly in Sequoia National Forest. Mountain streams feed Kern River, sole home to rare little kern golden trout. High mountain lakes, jagged granite peaks.

HOOVER 43,000 acres that cross into Toiyabe National Forest (Nevada). Rugged, heavily wooded slopes and steep canyons.

JOHN MUIR 584,000 acres extending more than 30 miles along the Sierra Nevada crest, partly in Sierra National Forest. Several 14,000-foot peaks, including Mt. Whitney, and 53 glaciers.

SOUTH SIERRA 63,000 acres shared by Sequoia National Forest. Lower elevations than other wilderness areas, but still marked by craggy, granite peaks. Lush meadows and wooded mountain ridges are popular hiking and riding destinations.

HIKING AND RIDING More than 1,200 miles of trails, including portions of the Pacific Crest Trail, lead to hundreds of waterfalls, glacial lakes, and meadows in the five wilderness areas. Many are open to horseback riders, and 13 guides run pack trains. Mountain bicycles permitted on some trails, but banned in the wilderness.

CAMPING Dispersed camping is allowed throughout much of the national forest, although restricted in the Mammoth Lakes area. Forest Service maintains 83 campgrounds with room for 12,000 people.

PICNICKING Allowed throughout the national forest, or stop at three designated sites near Mammoth, the Sierra vista near the Ancient Bristlecone Pine Forest, Mono Lake, Convict Lake, and Hot Creek.

ALPINE SKIING Two resorts can handle 21,000 people a day: Mammoth Mtn. (2 gondolas and 29 lifts) and June Lake (7 lifts).

CROSS-COUNTRY SKIING Wilderness hut-hopping gaining popularity. Groomed trails at Obsidian Dome, Rock Creek Canyon, and Tamarack Lodge and Sierra Meadows near Mammoth.

SCENIC DRIVES Hwy. 395 runs the 165-mile length of the national forest and yields spectacular views of the craggy eastern Sierra escarpment. Hwy. 168 from Big Pine to the Ancient Bristlecone Pine Forest is a narrow, winding tour through the rocky White Mountains; Sierra View looks across the valley at the Sierra highcountry from 9,000 feet.

HUNTING California Fish & Game license required. Prohibited in game refuges and Mammoth Lakes area. Seasons on deer, bear, smaller game, and birds.

FISHING California Fish & Game license required. Trout in most wilderness streams and lakes. Angler's parking lots give access to 10 lakes in the Mammoth Lakes Basin, as well as at Convict Lake, Mammoth Creek, Hot Creek, and Owens River. Hot Creek is a wild trout stream—barbless hooks, catch-and-release.

OFF-ROAD VEHICLES AND SNOWMOBILES Green stickers and spark arrestors required. Geography, geology, and the fact that much of the national forest is designated wilderness limit these activities to non-wilderness Forest Service roads.

ADMINISTRATIVE OFFICES

FOREST HEADQUARTERS 873 N. Main St., Bishop CA 93514 (619) 873-5841

MAMMOTH RANGER DISTRICT P.O. Box 148, Mammoth Lakes CA 93546 (619) 934-2505

MONO LAKE RANGER DISTRICT P.O. Box 429, Lee Vining CA (619) 647-6525

MT. WHITNEY RANGER DISTRICT P.O. Box 8, Lone Pine CA 93545 (619) 876-5542

WHITE MOUNTAIN RANGER DISTRICT 798 N. Main St., Bishop CA 93514 (619) 873-4207

TOIYABE
NATIONAL FOREST DIRECTORY

POINTS OF INTEREST

TWIN LAKES about 15 miles west of Bridgeport on Twin Lakes Road is popular with anglers and hikers. Four trailheads lead to Hoover Wilderness; other trails reach subalpine meadows and lakes.

RECREATION AREAS

BRIDGEPORT VALLEY Seven campgrounds, dozens of lakes and streams for fishing, four trailheads into Hoover Wilderness, Sonora Bridge Picnic Area off Hwy. 108, shooting banned, off-road vehicles allowed only on designated routes.

WILDERNESS AREAS

HOOVER 48,000 acres along the Sierra Nevada crest. Camp size limited to 25 peo-

ple, except eight at Sawtooth Ridge. Steep rugged country pocked with glacial lakes.

CARSON-ICEBERG 156,000 acres with about half on Carson Ranger District. Pacific Crest Trail loops along East Fork Carson River.

RECREATIONAL ACTIVITIES

HIKING AND RIDING Hundreds of miles of trails open to hikers, horseback riders, and mountain bicyclists.

CAMPING Allowed through the national forest and at 13 campgrounds maintained by the Forest Service.

PICNICKING Allowed throughout the national forest and at the Sonora Bridge day-use area.

ALPINE SKIING Slide Mtn. (2 lifts) off Hwy. 428, and Mt. Rose (5 Lifts) off Hwy. 50.

CROSS-COUNTRY SKIING Allowed on all hiking trails, some groomed trails at Tahoe Meadows five miles west of Incline Village, and in Hope Valley on Hwy. 88 east of Carson Pass.

SCENIC DRIVES Hwy. 395 north of Mono Lake climbs to Conway Summit with beautiful views of Mono Lake and the Bridgeport Valley.

FISHING Record-sized brook, brown, and rainbow trout have been caught in Twin Lakes area. Robinson Creek, the East and West Forks of the Walker River, and Bridgeport Reservoir are popular trout spots. California Fish & Game license required.

HUNTING California Fish & Game license required. Seasons on mule deer.

OFF-ROAD VEHICLES AND SNOWMOBILES Over 100 miles of backcountry forest roads in Bridgeport and Carson ranger districts open to ORVS and snowmobiles.

ADMINISTRATIVE OFFICES

FOREST HEADQUARTERS 1200 Franklin Way, Sparks, NV 89341 (702) 331-6444

BRIDGEPORT RANGER DISTRICT P.O. Box 595, Bridgeport, CA 93517 (619) 932-7070

CARSON RANGER DISTRICT 1536 S. Carson St., Carson City, NV 89701 (702) 882-2766

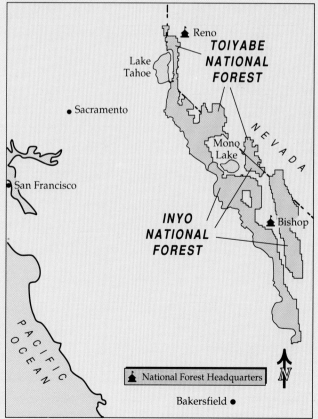

Granite boulders called glacial erratics are sprinkled throughout alpine meadows such as this one in the Pine Creek basin in the John Muir Wilderness. BARBARA BRUNDEGE

Sierra

Heavenly high country

In 1873, pioneer conservationist John Muir camped several days at the base of the Minarets, a series of jagged peaks that tower twelve thousand feet into the clear air of the Sierra Nevada. "Clad free as a Highlander" in the heat radiated by the black slabs, Muir climbed six glaciers in the nearby Ritter Basin. The father of the Sierra Club was so awed by raw avalanche scars and ice-sculpted canyons that he swore they spoke the very words of his God.

Today, the Minarets rise in Sierra National Forest, a vast, 1.3-million-acre section of divine, rugged country between Kings Canyon National Park on the south, Yosemite National Park on the north, and Inyo National Forest on the east. With elevations ranging from 900 feet to 13,986-foot Mt. Humphreys, Sierra National Forest contains chaparral slopes, grass- and woodland-covered foothills, hundreds of lakes and reservoirs, steep-walled canyons, dense forests, alpine meadows, and some of the highest, sharpest, most severely carved peaks in the Sierra Nevada.

These features lure four million visitors a year to Sierra National Forest, located 205 miles from San Francisco and 240 miles from Los Angeles. Most visitors arrive through Fresno on California Highway 168, the main road into the national forest. The highway provides access to sixty-four campgrounds, eleven major lakes, and five wilderness areas that cover forty-three percent of the national forest.

Roads may carry visitors to Sierra National Forest, but people return for the same reason that Western Piute Indians summered here and legions of utility company workers flooded the woods at the turn of the century—water. More than four hundred small lakes decorate Sierra's backcountry, while eleven large lakes in major valleys harness nature's raw energy to generate electricity. Channelized water roils through numerous dams and powerhouses built on parts of the San Joaquin and Kings rivers within the national forest.

The man-made and enlarged lakes in the national forest are popular recreation sites. Sailing regattas take place at Huntington Lake, while motorboats cruise Mammoth Pool, Pine Flat, Courtright, and Wishon reservoirs and Edison, Florence, Shaver, Kerckhoff, Bass and Redinger lakes. Visitors swim in many of the lakes and fish at most of them for golden, rainbow, and brook trout.

For all the dams and reservoirs, Sierra National Forest's many streams and rivers flow mostly undammed over boulder-lined beds. The main and south forks of the Merced and the middle and south forks of the Kings are wild and scenic rivers, flowing free for 224 miles along Sierra's north and south boundaries, making ideal whitewater for rafting and kayaking.

After it rolls out of Yosemite, the Merced River cuts the northwest corner of Sierra National Forest for about eleven miles. Rafters run the Merced in the spring when it is high with snow melt. By summer, hardcore river runners abandon the river to floaters in inner tubes who loll in the low water.

One of the national forest's most scenic drives is State Highway 140 where it follows the Merced River from El Portal to the foothill community of Briceburg. Eastbound drivers have stunning arroyo vistas. Westbound drivers gaze at the Pinochle Granite Ridge to the south.

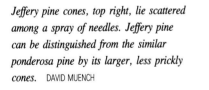

Jeffery pine cones, top right, lie scattered among a spray of needles. Jeffery pine can be distinguished from the similar ponderosa pine by its larger, less prickly cones. DAVID MUENCH

Kayakers and rafters shoot the Merced and Kings rivers on runs that range from Class III (moderate) to Class V (difficult) when the spring snows melt, right. GARY MOON

Bull Buck Tree, far right, dominates the Nelder Grove of giant sequoia in Sierra National Forest. A campground and self-guided nature trail occupy the grove, one of seventy that stretch from Placer County to Tulare County on the western slopes of the Sierra Nevada. BILL EVARTS

Like its national forest and national park neighbors, Sierra National Forest contains groves of giant sequoias. Highway 41 from Oakhurst provides access to Nelder Grove, where the one-mile, self-guided Shadow of the Giants Trail leads visitors not only past majestic sequoias but past immense white firs, sugar pines, and incense cedars. Even larger sequoias are found in the national forest's McKinley Grove southeast of Dinkey Creek.

In addition to these giants, Sierra National Forest contains one of the rarest shrubs in the country—carpenteria, a several-stemmed shrub that grows twice as tall as a man. The plant was discovered by explorer John C. Fremont in 1845 and only grows in a small area of chaparral near the national forest boundary along Highway 168. The Carpenteria Botanical Area deserves a visit in May and June when the shrubs produce their large white flowers.

Whatever the season, Highway 168 provides a spectacular, winding drive high into Sierra National Forest. The road passes numerous trailheads, campgrounds, picnic areas, and scenic views, starting with 7,832-foot Bald Mountain looming over the eastern shore of Shaver Lake. An extensive network of cross-country ski trails and snowmobile trails surrounds both Shaver Lake and Huntington Lake about seven miles farther east.

Highway 168 climbs nearly two thousand feet from Shaver Lake to Huntington Lake and on to Kaiser Pass. Along the way, sharp switchbacks and roadside pull-outs provide stupendous views of the Kaiser, Ansel Adams, and John Muir wilderness areas. Thick conifer forests fill the valleys while sheer formations with names like Bear Butte, Mount Torn, and Volcanic Knob jut serenely into the sky.

Five miles above Huntington, Highway 168 suddenly veers left on a narrow, enchanting twist up and over Kaiser Pass. An official sign marks the pass, but an enigmatic marker on the south side of the road might catch your eye instead: "Whiskey, Babe and Trim. Jerry Dwyer's dog team, 1920-25." The memorial honors three of the pack dogs that construction crews relied on to mush food and medical supplies over the pass during harsh winters. The dogs didn't die here—a sentimental Dwyer erected the memorial in honor of their hard work in mounting the pass.

Winters are severe and long in the country called the High Sierra beyond the pass. Heavy snows often blanket the land from mid-October through June. Summers—if defined as the period when the ground is frost free—are short, lasting only from mid-July through August when temperatures range from freezing to eighty-five degrees.

Four of Sierra National Forest's five wilderness areas—Ansel Adams, Dinkey Lakes, Kaiser, and John Muir—attract as many as ten thousand hikers, horseback riders, and climbers each season. Each must have a wilderness permit, and between July and October, a quota limits the number of overnight campers. The fifth wilderness area—Monarch—is steep, rugged terrain with few trails or visitors, but abundant solitude.

These wilderness areas offer a range of challenges from half-day loops to week-long, cross-country forays into the backcountry. High Sierra foresters call Humphreys Basin, a nob of the John Muir Wilderness that juts into the Kings Canyon National Park and Inyo National Forest, "moon with lakes" for good reason. The immense alpine area spreads across a barren granite floor pocked with glacial lakes. The John Muir and Pacific Crest trails merge and pass below The Pinnacles, razor-thin peaks that form the western boundary of the remote area. French Canyon and Piute Canyon trails penetrate the backcountry, but some experienced hikers prefer traveling cross-country to destinations such as Italy and Desolation lakes.

The three-mile hike from Bolsillo Campground to Corbett Lake in the John Muir Wilderness climbs two thousand feet through boulder fields, mixed stands of firs, pines, and incense cedars, and three alpine meadows. Hikers hear coyotes yowling at the rising sun and woodpeckers hammering at snags, and fishermen find trout in Corbett breaking the surface for slow-moving flies. Several other trails into the Ansel Adams and John Muir wilderness areas begin from Lake Edison and Florence Lake beyond the High Sierra Ranger Station.

Little wonder that High Sierra foresters call the basin below Mt. Humphreys "moon with lakes," left. The remote meadows and granite fields are pocked with cirques such as Desolation Lake, which reflects the 13,986-foot peak in an evening glow.
PAT O' HARA

AN ANCIENT TRADITION

In a tradition that archaeologists think might be five thousand years old, Mono and Chuckchansi Indians return to Mono Hot Springs in Sierra National Forest every summer for a spiritual cleansing. The ceremony is symbolic for some Mono elders, but they follow the tradition to keep attuned to their culture—and for fun.

Margaret Baty, a local Mono, says her grandparents stopped at the springs after traveling over Mono Pass, near Mt. Starr, to trade acorns for pinyon pine nuts with other Indians. Now Baty and other Mono elders drive to the springs each year "for a barbecue and all that goes with it, and just to keep the culture alive," she says.

The springs are a tonic to any visitor. From the Mono Springs resort, cross the *south fork of the San Joaquin River on a plank and scramble up the hillside to a meadow, where several concrete tubs await you. The lowest spring is the warmest. The Civilian Conservation Corps built the tubs in the 1930s.*

The area is sometimes called an "attractive nuisance" because the soggy meadow is trampled and muddied from people searching for unlined springs and because unthinking bathers leave litter in the area. Nonetheless, the springs continue to attract travelers who find the combination of warm water, the nearby San Joaquin River, and the surrounding trees and meadows a pleasant experience.

All the High Sierra trails skim over a carpet of brilliant wildflowers that begin to bloom as the snow first melts in the spring and fade as the first snow flies in the fall. Snowplant's bright red blossoms burn through the last vestiges of snow like low-lying torches marking the onset of spring. Through the summer, lavender pussypaws rise to the sun each morning and droop in the evening, creamy mariposa lilies bloom, and delicate orange and red columbine hang head-down in the breeze. As the weather cools, rabbitbrush bursts yellow along the roadside until crisp winds that herald the first snows of winter crash against the mountains.

Heeding the warning, Sierra National Forest rangers abandon the High Sierra and close the steep Kaiser Pass road before they are snowed in, stopping at switchbacks to ponder the messages of the Minarets as they rise in volcanic splendor some thirty-five miles to the north.

When its twisted, serrated blooms slice through the melting slush, snow plant heralds the beginning of spring in the High Sierra. JEFF FOOTT

THE HARDEST WORKING WATER IN THE WORLD

Gifford Pinchot, the first chief of the Forest Service, had few doubts about using mountain streams to generate electricity. He approved what he thought brought the most benefit to the most people.

So it was that crews from Pacific Light and Power Co. (later bought by Southern California Edison Co.) marched into the High Sierra in 1911 to build the first of eight powerhouses, six dams, and six lakes in Sierra National Forest. The work continued through 1988, when a powerhouse at Shaver Lake opened. Pacific Gas and Electric Co. runs another two dams and powerhouses in the High Sierra.

Together, the complex system of reservoirs, dams, and powerhouses use and reuse the San Joaquin River and its tributaries to generate electricity for more than one million homes in California. Few streams anywhere pass through so many power-producing structures in such a short distance, prompting hydroelectric engineers to call these streams the hardest working water in the world.

The systems follow a basic principle—gravity. From the dam on Mono Creek that created Lake Edison to Redinger Lake on the San Joaquin below, the water Edison uses drops more than eight thousand feet. It is collected and rerouted through at least six of the eight powerhouses in its chain. Water stored at Mammoth Pool is routed separately before joining the chain. All the water falls into Millerton Reservoir on the San Joaquin, where it is dispersed for irrigation in the valley below.

Visitors can get a feel for this water's energy by touring the Big Creek powerhouse. Call Camp Edison for details.

SIERRA
NATIONAL FOREST DIRECTORY

P O I N T S   O F   I N T E R E S T

BIG CREEK DAM AND POWERHOUSE Tours arranged by contacting Southern California Edison at Camp Edison, P.O. Box 6, Shaver Lake 93664, or call (209) 841-3444.

MONO HOT SPRINGS In the High Sierra off Kaiser Pass Rd., near Lake Edison.

KAISER PASS On Kaiser Pass Road, east of Huntington Lake.

MILE-HIGH VISTA South of Mammoth Pool Reservoir. Excellent view of Sierra Nevada.

R E C R E A T I O N   A R E A S

BASS LAKE Fishing, 12 campgrounds, 6 picnic grounds, a boat ramp, and trailheads. Contact Mariposa ranger station for fee and reservation information. Off county road 274, west of Oakhurst.

DINKEY CREEK Fishing, 6 campgrounds, trailheads, private resorts, and a pack station scattered around the confluence of six streams. Contact Dinkey Creek ranger station for fee and reservation information. On Dinkey Creek Rd., east of Shaver Lake.

HUNTINGTON LAKE Eight campgrounds, picnic area, backcountry pack station, boat ramp, trailheads, private resorts, and nearby Sierra Summit alpine ski resort. Fishing, sailing, swimming on the lake. Contact Pineridge ranger station for fee and reservation information. Off Hwy. 168, east of Fresno.

KINGS RIVER SPECIAL MANAGEMENT AREA Split between the Sierra and Sequoia national forests. Twelve campgrounds and a picnic ground between the Monarch Wilderness and Pine Flat Reservoir. White-water rafting, fishing, and hiking. Contact Kings River ranger station for fee and reservation information.

SHAVER LAKE Two campgrounds, two boat ramps, plus a recreation complex run by Southern California Edison. Fishing, swimming, waterskiing, and nordic skiing. Contact Pineridge ranger station and Edison for fee and reservation information.

W I L D E R N E S S   A R E A S

Free entry permits required for all wildernesses. Quotas restrict visitors to Ansel Adams, Dinkey Lakes, John Muir, and Kaiser from July 1 through Labor Day. Ranger stations distribute applications.

ANSEL ADAMS 228,500 acres of granite peaks and steep gorges at elevations to 13,157 feet. Small glaciers on north- and east-facing high peaks. Dominated by the Minarets and Ritter ranges. Headwaters of the North and Middle forks of the San Joaquin River. Partly on Inyo National Forest.

DINKEY LAKES 30,000 acres of lodgepole pine stands interrupted by meadows, rock outcroppings, and 16 glacial lakes.

JOHN MUIR 584,000 acres of snow-capped mountains, glaciers, cirques, and meadows along the Sierra Nevada crest from Mammoth Lakes to Mt. Whitney. Lower elevations covered with Jeffrey and lodgepole pine, incense cedar, white and red fir.

KAISER 23,000 acres on both sides of the Kaiser Ridge. Alpine meadows and lakes to the north, dense fir and pine forest on the south.

MONARCH 45,000 acres of steep, rugged slopes on Sierra and Sequoia national forests.

R E C R E A T I O N A L   A C T I V I T I E S

HIKING AND RIDING More than 1,100 miles of trails open to hikers, horseback riders, and mountain bicyclists. 30 miles of Pacific Crest Trail, Black Point and Rancheria Falls National Recreation Trails, Garnet Dike Trail along wild and scenic Kings River, and Shadow of the Giants, a one-mile, self-guided tour through giant sequoia. Campfire permits required.

CAMPING Allowed throughout the forest at 73 campgrounds.

PICNICKING Allowed throughout out the forest, or try one of 17 designated day-use areas—many in recreation areas.

ALPINE SKIING Seven lifts at Sierra Summit near Huntington Lake.

CROSS-COUNTRY SKIING Allowed on most forest backcountry roads. Some groomed or marked trails at Sierra Summit resort; Huntington Lake and Tamarack Ridge, on Hwy. 168; Goat Meadow, south of Yosemite National Park; and Shaver Lake, on Hwy. 168.

WHITE-WATER RAFTING AND KAYAKING On two wild and scenic rivers. Ten-mile run, rated Class III-V (moderate to difficult) on upper Kings River. Merced River, on northern fringe of forest, runs low by summer.

SCENIC DRIVES Hwy. 168 climbs from hazy San Joaquin Valley to fresh, fragrant pine, fir, and cedar forests, passing Shaver and Huntington lakes. Kaiser Pass Rd. is a narrow paved road past sheer rock outcroppings and glacial erratics, views of the Minarets and High Sierra.

HUNTING California Fish & Game license required. Seasons on mule deer, black bear, squirrels, quail, and rabbit.

FISHING California Fish & Game license required. Eleven major reservoirs, hundreds of wilderness and high country lakes, and miles of streams with rainbow and brown trout. Parking and boat launches at recreation areas.

OFF-ROAD VEHICLES AND SNOWMOBILES Green stickers and spark arrestors required. Allowed on backcountry roads; banned from wilderness. Four designated routes near wilderness areas: Spanish, west of John Muir; Swamp and Brewer, west of Dinkey Lakes; and Dusy, between Dinkey Lakes and Muir. Snowmobile routes at Huntington Lake, Tamarack Ridge, and Whiskey Lake.

A D M I N I S T R A T I V E   O F F I C E S

FOREST HEADQUARTERS 1130 O St., Fresno CA 93721 (209) 487-5155

DINKEY RANGER DISTRICT (summer only) Dinkey Rte., Shaver Lake CA 93664 (209) 841-3404

KINGS RIVER RANGER DISTRICT 34849 Maxon Rd., Sanger CA 93657 (209) 855-8321

MARIPOSA RANGER DISTRICT 41969 Highway 41, Oakhurst CA 93644 (209) 683-4665

MINARETS RANGER DISTRICT North Fork CA 93643 (209) 877-2218

PINERIDGE RANGER DISTRICT P.O. Box 300, Shaver Lake CA 93664 (209) 841-3311

Remnants of the gold-rush era, such as this miner's wheel resting in a field of poppies, are scattered throughout the national forests in California's Mother Lode country. Prospecters still sluice, pan, and dredge for gold in forest streams. DAVID MUENCH

Stanislaus and Eldorado

N A T I O N A L   F O R E S T S

Searching for the Mother Lode

From 1848 to 1882, thousands of men and women sluiced, panned, and dug for gold in countless canyons, valleys, and streams along the central Sierra Nevada, in and around what would later become the Stanislaus and Eldorado national forests.

Thousands of wagon trains clattered over the area's Mormon-Emigrant Trail, Sonora Pass, Fremont-Carson Route, and Luther Pass.

Nancy Kelsey was the first American woman to make the Sierra Nevada crossing into California, coming barefoot over the Sonora Pass in 1841 when she was a 17-year-old mother.

When the gold rush moved to Bodie on the east side of the Sierra Nevada, argonauts climbed the same passes from west to east in search of their fortunes. Several national forest roads and hiking trails follow these same paths, and wagon ruts remain visible in places.

The forested mountains and valleys provided timber for hastily built mining towns, but most of the towns busted as quickly as they boomed. Today, a half-dozen state parks on the perimeter of the national forests preserve the best evidence of the Gold Rush era.

Although the gold era is gone, Eldorado and Stanislaus national forests continue to produce valuable commodities—water, electricity, timber, and seedlings—and provide the nearest Sierra Nevada playgrounds for about ten million people from Sacramento, Stockton, and San Francisco.

Dams on several forest rivers trap water for the cities and turn turbines that generate electricity for homes and businesses in central California. Loggers cut enough fir and Jeffrey, sugar, and ponderosa pine to supply building materials for 20,000 three-bedroom houses a year. The felled trees are replaced each spring by more than fifteen million seedlings grown at the Forest Service's Placerville Nursery.

Nearly twenty-five national forest reservoirs are popular sites for fishing, swimming, and boating.

Backcountry fishermen trek to dozens of glacial lakes that harbor trout, and wildlife watchers scan the skies for endangered bald eagles and peregrine falcons, and other birds of prey such as goshawks, spotted owls, and ospreys. These and other recreational activities lure pleasure-seekers rather than gold-seekers into Stanislaus and Eldorado national forests.

STANISLAUS
N A T I O N A L   F O R E S T

One of the oldest national forests in America, Stanislaus National Forest orginally was part of the Stanislaus Forest Reserve created in 1897. The reserve was huge, encompassing all or part of what later became five national forests—Stanislaus, Sierra, Eldorado, Tahoe, and Toiyabe. The reserve drew its name from the Stanislaus River, which was named to honor Estanislaus, a Miwok Indian who led an 1828 revolt against mission padres and lived free for seven years before surrendering.

Today, the 900,000-acre Stanislaus National Forest stretches between the Mokelumne River on the north and the Merced River on the south. Its eastern border is formed by Yosemite National Park and Toiyabe National Forest. Two recreation areas, two alpine ski resorts, and the Tuolumne River attract many of Stanislaus National Forest's present-day visitors.

The Tuolumne River flows free for twenty-eight wild

and scenic miles through the national forest's southern flank. Rafters and kayakers float the river from May through October, and Highway 120 parallels the river through much of the rugged Jawbone Ridge backcountry.

North of Tuolumne River and almost in the middle of the national forest along Highway 108, Pinecrest Recreation Area provides a popular spot for a wide variety of year-round recreation. The area contains two family campgrounds with room for three hundred tents, four group camps, two nature trails, a boat launch, marina, and swimming beach. In the winter, skiers pass through Pinecrest on their way to the Dodge Ridge Ski Area, while snowmobilers and cross-country skiers take to separate paths marked all around the area.

It is easy to understand the area's appeal. Tall pine and cedars shade the campgrounds and ring the reservoir. Summer temperatures rarely exceed the mid-80s even when the nearby Central Valley bakes in 100-degree heat.

The Tuolumne River, right, runs free through the Stanislaus National Forest for twenty-eight miles between the Hetch Hetchy Reservoir in Yosemite National Park and the Don Pedro Reservoir in the Central Valley. The river has earned "wild and scenic" status and legions of whitewater enthusiasts brave its rapids from May through September. RON SANFORD

Deer abound in California national forests, far right. Fall brings hunting season for those with California licenses, but this doe and fawn are off-limits—only bucks can be taken. JEFF FOOTT

Dependable winter snowfall—as much as fifty inches per year—falls on the nearby peaks. Short, easy nature hikes throughout the area tell of Miwok life and the silent battle between individual trees and species for sunlight, water, and dominance of an area.

Many of the area's colorful stories come to life on a Forest Service cassette tape. The tape, available at the Pinecrest Ranger Station, guides motorists on a two-hour sojourn over Sonora Pass on Highway 108. Narrated by Stanislaus National Forest interpretive specialist Gary Hines, the tape provides an amusing account of gold miners' water battles and rough-and-tumble logging camps.

The tape notes features that show how the Sierra Nevada was formed. Massive uplifting some nine million years ago tilted the range, which was then sculpted by volcanoes and glaciers. From Donnell Vista, travelers see the volcanic Dardanelles, three peaks rising over 8,800 feet in the national forest's Carson-Iceberg Wilderness. The Dardanelles are the last, eroded vestiges of an ancient lava flow that once filled the Stanislaus Valley.

The Sonora Pass route eventually climbs to Chipmunk Flat, an alpine meadow filled with wildflowers in the spring and golden quaking aspen in the fall. The flat lies below Sonora Pass, and pioneers who struggled over the pass and finally reached this vibrant mountain meadow must have whooped for joy at the pleasant contrast it provided with the harsh peaks around it, including the barren, blue Excelsior Mountains of Toiyabe National Forest visible to the east from atop the pass.

Sonora Pass marks a five-mile gap between 11,750-foot Leavitt Peak in Emigrant Wilderness and 11,462-foot Sonora Peak in Carson-Iceberg Wilderness. The wilderness areas are as distinct as they are close. Emigrant is High Sierra country marked by volcanic ridges, alpine meadows, and dozens of glacial lakes. Carson-Iceberg is a dry, granitic wilderness that rises over the Lake Alpine Recreation Area and receives fewer backcountry trekkers than the Emigrant Wilderness.

The Lake Alpine Recreation Area features six campgrounds, three picnic areas, a boat ramp, two trails for hikers and horses and one for off-road vehicles, and the Mt. Reba Ski Area. There is quiet late-season camping, nordic skiing at Bear Valley, and wilderness alpine skiing in the nearby Mukelumne Wilderness, an area that extends from Stanislaus National Forest into adjacent Eldorado National Forest.

Eldorado National Forest was carved from the Stanislaus National Forest in 1910 in part to give foresters more local control over cattle grazing and railroad logging operations.

For decades, ranchers grazed their cattle—and sold dairy products to weary travelers coming over the passes—in the mountain meadows while loggers used narrow-gauge railroads to climb into the Sierra Nevada for ponderosa and Jeffrey pine. These industries continue today, although logging trucks and roads have replaced locomotives and steel rails.

Logging takes place on national forest land and on private land around Lookout Mountain. Cattle grazing continues on extensive private land in Union Valley, along with national forest land. In all, about twenty percent of the land within the borders of Eldorado National Forest is privately owned.

The national forest's high country remains relatively wild, however. Deer, black bear, and the rare Sierra red fox roam in game refuges tucked into pockets on Eldorado's north and south sides. The Mokelumne Wilderness covers almost ten percent of the forest on the southwest corner, and the popular Desolation Wilderness lays on another ten percent at the forest's northeast side.

Mokelumne's rugged backcountry is dominated by massive, stark granite domes and spires like 10,380-foot Round Top and 9,332-foot Mokelumne Peak. Summit City Creek cuts north and south through the wilderness. One trail follows the creek for fifteen miles from Camp Irene to a tumbling water-

fall at Horse Canyon and out to Elephant's Back in the Toiyabe National Forest. Trailheads from the north are scattered along Highway 88, the first National Forest Scenic Byway in California.

Desolation Wilderness contains high, alpine meadows and dozens of small glacial lakes squeezed between the east face of the Sierra Nevada, known locally as the Crystal Range, and Lake Tahoe. Easy to find and moderately difficult to hike, the wilderness has been popular since it was created as a primitive reserve in 1931. By 1971, increasing use damaged some backcountry areas, and a camping quota of seven

A field of wildflowers awaits springtime visitors to the Mother Lode country in the Eldorado National Forest. DAVID MUENCH

hundred people a night was imposed.

Eleven campgrounds, five lakes, four boat ramps, three picnic grounds, and miles of off-road vehicle and hiking trails are bunched in fir and pine forest on the west side of the Crystal Range. Just north of Highway 50, which follows the old Pony Express route, the Crystal Basin Recreation Area became popular after the Sacramento Municipal Utility District in 1957 built a series of dams and created Loon Lake, Gerle Reservoir, Union Valley Reservoir, and Ice House Reservoir. In the winter, ORV trails are open to snowmobiles while nordic skiers take to hiking trails, especially at Loon Lake. Robbs Hut, eight miles southwest of Loon, is a rebuilt fire lookout bunkhouse available by reservation.

Loggers cut enough red fir, Douglas-fir, sugar pine, and Jeffery pine from the Eldorado and Stanislaus national forests to build about 20,000 three-bedroom houses a year. TOM MYERS

T O M O R R O W ' S   F O R E S T S

Locked away at zero degrees, wrapped in plastic bags, placed in cardboard boxes, and stacked on metal shelves, tomorrow's national forests slumber in peace.

An estimated seventy thousand pounds of seeds from every species of pine and fir that grows in the California national forests are stored in a warehouse-size cooler at Placerville Nursery, a part of Eldorado National Forest. Each year, about 6,000 pounds of seeds become fifteen million seedlings destined for replanting in the national forests. Some of the young trees replace majestic stands consumed by fire. Most go into timber areas that were logged the preceeding years and will be logged again in 80 to 120 years when the seedlings have grown into timber-sized trees.

Each fall, foresters throughout California harvest ripe cones and separate them into lots according to species, elevation, and geographical location. The lots are trucked to the nursery, where workers sort and place them in screen-bottomed trays.

The trays are stacked in a drying room where warm air wafts over the cones, triggering them to open and release the

seeds. Sparrows dart among the trays, feasting on bugs that would otherwise eat the seeds.

The seeds are collected and run through a series of machines that husks the seeds' wings and separates the good seeds from the bad. Then it's off to the cooler where the seeds will repose until planted.

Most seeds wait five to ten years before they are planted, twenty-eight seedlings per square foot, across much of the nursery's

157 acres. Late in the winter, the foot-tall seedlings are dug from the ground and packed in large paper bags—eight hundred seedlings to a bag. In early spring, the seedlings are trucked to the national forests and planted, five hundred per acre. The planting is successful if three hundred trees per acre survive all the hazards of weather, insects, disease, and browsing wild animals to reach maturity.

TOM MYERS

Four downhill ski resorts take advantage of the seven-foot snowpack that often covers high country slopes for up to six months a year. The resorts—Sierra Ski Ranch, Kirkwood Meadows, Echo Summit, and Iron Mountain—offer good skiing at a more peaceful pace than the nearby Lake Tahoe slopes.

Summer in Eldorado National Forest is short, cool, and dry. Temperatures from mid-July through September range from 35 to 95 degrees. The higher elevations are cooler and wetter than the foothills. Snow sometimes doesn't disappear before August and sudden thunderstorms can materialize in just a few hours. ■

THE SMALLEST NATIONAL FOREST

It is not easy to hide giant sequoia. The bulkiest trees on earth can live 3,500 years, grow 270 feet tall, and spread one hundred feet around at their bases.

So why is Calaveras Big Trees National Forest one of California's best-kept secrets? A famous neighbor, the Calaveras Big Trees State Park, gets all the attention. The state park surrounds the national forest on three sides and lures thousands of tourists each year to see "Big Stump," the 24-foot wide stub of Discovery Tree, a giant felled in 1853 by misguided opportunists.

Meanwhile, Calaveras Big Trees National Forest is so tiny—only 360 acres—and so obscure that it isn't counted in the tally of national forests in California. Officially, it is a full-fledged forest, but for all practical purposes, Calaveras is the ward of Stanislaus National Forest, making it a forest-within-a-forest.

No trees are cut in Calaveras, and the lone trail through the area is overtaken by wildflowers. Other than botany students who make occasional forays through the sequoia groves, the land is untrammeled by humans.

STANISLAUS
NATIONAL FOREST DIRECTORY

P O I N T S   O F   I N T E R E S T

MI-WUK VILLAGE on Hwy. 108 at the national forest's west entrance is a restored Native American town that depicts the area's earliest history.
HIGHWAY 108 climbs to Sonora Pass, a barren, windy point that looks east to Great Basin ranges and west into the woods and meadows of the national forest.
CALAVERAS BIG TREES NATIONAL FOREST is a separate national forest, but the tiny 360-acre stand of giant sequoia is managed by Stanislaus foresters. Only one trail traverses the primitive area.
TUOLUMNE RIVER is a wild and scenic river.

R E C R E A T I O N   A R E A S

LAKE ALPINE Six campgrounds, three picnic grounds, boat ramp, marina and resort, hiking and equestrian trailheads. Lake and stream fishing at 7,000 feet; Mt.Reba alpine ski resort near. On Hwy. 4, at tip of Carson-Iceberg Wilderness.
PINECREST Eight campgrounds, a picnic ground, beach, boat ramp, marina, and hiking trailheads. Fishing, swimming, and sailing on Pinecrest Lake; amphitheater at lakeside where foresters present nature and history programs in the summer. Dodge Ridge alpine ski resort nearby.

W I L D E R N E S S   A R E A S

CARSON-ICEBERG 160,000 acres dominated by volcanic ridges and the crest of the Sierra Nevada at the northeast corner of the national forest.
EMIGRANT 112,000 acres of glaciated western slopes of the central Sierra Nevada, dominated by volcanic peaks to the north and lakes and meadows to the south. The area was traveled by argonauts after the discovery of gold in California in 1848.
MOKELUMNE 49,500 acres mostly in Eldorado National Forest. Stanislaus portion contains North Fork Mokelumne, with Blue Hole, a sparkling pool noted for good fishing.

R E C R E A T I O N A L   A C T I V I T I E S

HIKING AND RIDING 663 miles open to hikers, riders, and mountain bicyclists. Pacific Crest Trail traverses wilderness areas for 32 miles; 7 self-guided nature trails explain early Native American life, a natural bonsai garden of dwarf trees, and the formation of giant lava cliffs.
CAMPING Allowed throughout the national forest and at 47 campgrounds maintained by the Forest Service.
PICNICKING Allowed throughout the national forest and at 13 designated day-use areas at recreation areas, scenic vistas, and streamsides.
ALPINE SKIING Two resorts, Dodge Ridge (3 rope tows), just east of Pinecrest, and Mt.Reba (9 lifts), just north of Lake Alpine.
CROSS-COUNTRY SKIING on many backcountry roads. Groomed or marked trails at Pinecrest on Hwy. 108 and on meadows along Hwy. 4 near Bear Valley.
WHITE-WATER RAFTING AND KAYAKING May through October on 18-mile stretch of Tuolumne River between Lumsden Campground and Don Pedro Reservoir. Contact Groveland Ranger District for list of certified outfitters and permit information.
SCENIC DRIVES Hwy. 108 from Mi-wuk Village to Sonora Pass is two-hours through pine-, fir-, and cedar-forests. A Forest Service tape available at Pinecrest Ranger Station narrates the trip and describes highlights from glacial erratics to historic travelers.
HUNTING California Fish & Game license required. Seasons on mule deer, black bear, and wild turkey.
FISHING California Fish & Game license required. Emigrant Wilderness lakes and streams contain trout. Basin, Beaver, Deadman, Mocassin, and Clark Fork creeks, Lyons Reservoir, and the Stanislaus and Tuolumne Rivers are stocked with trout.
OFF-ROAD VEHICLES AND SNOWMOBILES Green stickers and spark arrestors required. Allowed on some backcountry roads; banned at Pinecrest and Dodge Ridge. Snowmobile routes at Lilly Creek, Cow Creek, and Donnell Vista off Hwy. 108 and at Alpine Basin and Spicer Road off Hwy. 4.

A D M I N I S T R A T I V E   O F F I C E S

FOREST HEADQUARTERS 19777 Greenley Rd., Sonora CA 95370 (209) 532-3671
CALAVERAS RANGER DISTRICT P.O. Box 500, Hathaway Pines CA 95233 (209) 795-1381

GROVELAND RANGER DISTRICT P.O. Box 75G, Groveland CA 95321 (209) 962-7825

MI-WOK RANGER DISTRICT P.O. Box 100, Mi-wuk Village CA 95346 (209) 586-3234

SUMMIT RANGER DISTRICT Star Rte, Box 1295, Sonora CA 95370 (209) 965-3434

ELDORADO
NATIONAL FOREST DIRECTORY

POINTS OF INTEREST

PLACERVILLE NURSERY off Hwy. 50 at Camino ships about 15 million pine and fir seedlings a year to northern California national forests for replanting after timber harvests and fires. Volunteers lead free guided tours, check for times at the Eldorado Information Center.

RECREATION AREAS

CRYSTAL BASIN Lying under the western rim of the Crystal Range. Includes five reservoirs, eight campgrounds, four picnic grounds, five boat ramps and trailheads to Desolation Wilderness. Swimming, canoeing, and water skiing are allowed on some lakes; snowmobile and nordic skiing are popular winter sports. Access from Ice House and Wrights Lake roads off Hwy. 50.

STUMPY MEADOWS and **HELL HOLE** Includes two reservoirs with six campgrounds, a picnic area, two boat ramps, hiking, horseback, and ORV trails. Fishing and boating very popular. Take Wentworth Springs Rd. to Stumpy Meadows, then Eleven Pines Rd. to Hell Hole.

WILDERNESS AREAS

DESOLATION 63,400 acres with hiker quotas on most trails. Check with rangers for reservation information. Trails climb from 6,500 to 10,000 feet, past small lakes, glacial moraines, stands of Jeffery and lodgepole pine and into alpine meadows.

MOKELUMNE 105,000 acres marked by granite domes and steep, wooded canyons and extends into Stanislaus and Toiyabe national forests.

RECREATIONAL ACTIVITIES

HIKING AND RIDING 460 miles of trails open to hikers and horseback riders. Trails loop into Crystal Basin or climb into the Sierra and wilderness areas. Sudden storms are common in the high country. Most roads outside wilderness areas are open to mountain bikers; check with ranger districts for restrictions.

CAMPING Permitted throughout the national forest and at 28 campgrounds the Forest Service maintains. Contact rangers for fee and reservation information.

PICNICKING Permitted throughout the national forest and at Cleveland Corral, Ice House, Fashoda, and Loon Lake designated picnic grounds in the Crystal Basin

ALPINE SKIING Four resorts, with a total capacity of 15,200 skiers a day: Iron Mtn. (5 lifts) and Kirkwood (10 lifts) are off Hwy. 89, Sierra Ski Ranch (10 lifts) and Echo Summit (3 lifts) are off Hwy. 50.

CROSS-COUNTRY SKIING In addition to groomed areas at alpine resorts, popular areas include Loon Lake, with nearby Robb's Hut available for overnight stays by reservation only; Lumberyard Trail, Peddler Hill, Leek Springs Loop, and Winnemucca Lake Loop along Hwy. 88; Strawberry Canyon; Bear River Lake Resort 22 miles east of Pioneer on Hwy. 88; and Cody Hut near Strawberry on Hwy. 50.

SCENIC DRIVES Hwy. 88 was the first National Scenic Byway in California. The road winds and climbs through pine and fir forests, with turnouts for views of Sierra granite escarpments at Peddler Hill and Shot Rock and Devil's Garden vistas. The road continues past lakes and ski resorts before crossing the Sierra at Carson Pass and dropping into Hope Valley enroute to Lake Tahoe.

HUNTING California Fish & Game license required. Prohibited in two state game refuges at the northwest and southwest corners of the national forest. Seasons on bear, deer, and a variety of smaller animals and birds.

FISHING California Fish & Game license required. Limits vary by location and season on 620 miles of streams and rivers, most have trout. Most reservoirs within the national forest have parking lots for anglers; streamside fishermen can park in marked turnouts or on road shoulders, where permitted.

OFF-ROAD VEHICLES AND SNOWMOBILES Green stickers and spark arrestors required. Most backcountry roads are open to four-wheel drive vehicles except closed in the winter and early spring. Fire restrictions during high or extreme fire danger may limit ORV use. Snowmobile trails at Loon Lake in the Crystal Basin, Bear River Reservoir, and permitted on many backcountry roads.

ADMINISTRATIVE OFFICES

FOREST HEADQUARTERS 100 Forni Rd., Placerville CA 95667 (916) 622-5061

ELDORADO INFORMATION CENTER 3070 Camino Heights Dr., Camino CA 95709 (916) 644-6048

AMADOR RANGER DISTRICT 26820 Silver Dr., Pioneer CA 95666 (209) 295-4251

GEORGETOWN RANGER DISTRICT 7600 Wentworth Springs, Georgetown CA 95634 (916) 333-4312

PLACERVILLE RANGER DISTRICT 3491 Carson Ct., Placerville CA 95667 (916) 644-2324

PACIFIC RANGER DISTRICT Hwy. 50, Pollock Pines CA 95726 (916) 644-2349

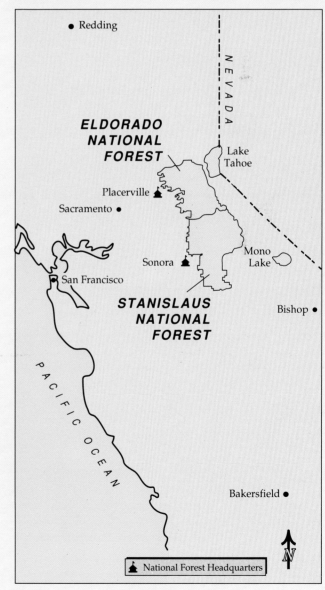

Day begins in Emerald Bay on Lake Tahoe, which was carved by glaciers that also formed Fallen Leaf and Cascade lakes in the surrounding mountains. LARRY ULRICH

Tahoe, Plumas and Lake Tahoe Basin

N A T I O N A L   F O R E S T S

Crown and jewel of the Sierra Nevada

Lake Tahoe sparkles like a teal jewel on the Sierra Nevada ridges that crown Tahoe and Plumas national forests and the Lake Tahoe Basin Management Unit. Together, these national forests strike a regal balance between work and play, the wild and the tame.

The basin surrounding the famous lake provides a year-round playground for skiers, hikers, fishermen, and boaters. Huge resorts rim the lake and cater to thousands of guests, many of whom visit the national forests for outdoor recreation.

Of course, not all activity takes place around the lake. Tahoe and Plumas national forests spread across the northern end of the Sierra Nevada from the Sacramento Valley on the east to the Cascade Range in the north. Along the way, they encompass numerous scenic roads and campgrounds, three wilderness areas, and two wild and scenic rivers.

Timber sales and power generation take place within each forest. Many reservoirs hold stream flows for power production, and many areas that were heavily logged in the late 1800s are now yielding a second timber harvest.

In all, the lake management unit and the two national forests offer visitors a wonderful look at some of California's most beautiful and productive country.

Skiers at Homewood, one of more than a dozen downhill ski resorts in the mountains that ring Lake Tahoe. FRANK S. BALTHIS

In 1844, explorer John Fremont stumbled upon a huge lake high in the Sierra Nevada that local Washoe Indians called Tahoe, meaning "big water." At the time, the 21-mile-long lake was incredibly clear, just like it had been for twenty-five million years since it first filled a basin between the Carson and Sierra ranges.

Development around Lake Tahoe started in the mid-1800s with the discovery of gold in the Sierra Nevada and silver at Nevada's Virginia City. The Bonanza Highway—today's Highway 50—connected Sacramento to Virginia City via Lake Tahoe, and by the 1870s, Lake Tahoe was one of the world's premiere resorts. Although today's skiers and gamblers are mostly middle-class, the original vacationers were elite San Franciscans who built lavish lakeside summer estates. Portions of three mansions at the Tallac Historic Site on the south shore have been refurbished, providing rustic venues for jazz concerts, art shows, and weddings.

Early timber companies cleared much of what later became Tahoe and Toiyabe national forests to build mines and houses. They left denuded slopes that sloughed into the lake, leaving an indelible imprint in the crystalline water. Rapid urbanization following World War II further clouded the lake.

Lake Tahoe still looks beautifully clear to most visitors, but early promoters boasted the lake was so clear a white dinner plate could be seen two hundred feet below the surface. Today that same white plate is visible eighty-nine feet deep.

To stop the dirty tide, two special government agencies were created. One is a California-Nevada planning group that regulates environmental standards for development around the border lake. To coordinate national forest efforts, the Forest Service in 1973 combined lands previously divided among the Tahoe, Toiyabe, and Eldorado national forests to create the Lake Tahoe Basin Management Unit. The unit spreads over two states and six counties.

Forest Service watershed specialists concentrate on reducing erosion from seventy streams and dozens of hillsides in the area, including ski slopes at sixteen ski resorts. However, much of this critical work goes unnoticed by the twenty-two million people who come here from throughout the world each year. Seven thousand motel rooms dot the south shore alone, and dozens of casinos operate on the Nevada side of the lake.

With a 350-inch average snow falls each winter, the basin accommodates the largest concentration of alpine ski resorts in the nation. They include large complexes such as Heavenly Valley, which rises to 10,067 feet at Monument Peak and covers slopes in two states, and Squaw Valley, site of the 1960 Winter Olympics. Eight nordic ski areas groom trails in the mountain meadows.

The basin is more than a ski area. Fallen Leaf Lake and Echo Lake in the Lake Tahoe Basin Management Unit are nestled into the back side of the Crystal Range above Lake Tahoe. Both offer fishing, boating, and trailheads into the Desolation Wilderness, which spreads from the unit into Eldorado National Forest. The high granite country is marked by steep crags, moraines, and hundreds of glacial lakes. A free permit is needed to enter the wilderness, and overnight camping is limited.

The Forest Service's Lake Tahoe Visitor Center sits amidst a huge south-shore recreation complex that includes a lakeside restaurant and resort, boat launches, swimming beaches, campgrounds, the historic Tallac mansions, and a Forest Service outdoor amphitheater for interpretive programs. Five short, self-guided nature trails describe Washoe Indian culture and early settlers' days, how trees grow, fire prevention, and the annual October run of the lake's kokanee salmon. The center includes an underground viewing chamber that allows visitors to see trout, salmon, and other aquatic life swimming in Taylor Creek.

For a nominal fee, the visitor center also provides a free cassette tape for people making the 76-mile drive around the lake. The tape narrates the scenic trip and recounts local lore about early lake history, Vikingsholm Castle, and Maggie's Peaks, the snowy cross that is said only to melt from Mt. Tallac in advance of a drought.

The forested slopes rimming Lake Tahoe's Emerald Bay are peppered with summer homes built before strict regulations were adopted to limit development and protect the clear waters. PAT O'HARA

Almost a third of the 1.2 million acres within Tahoe National Forest are privately owned, making the national forest map look like a giant checkerboard of one-mile sections of public and private land. The private lands are vestiges from the late 1800s when the federal government gave land to railroads, power companies, timber companies, and other commercial interests to encourage western development.

Other frontier history marks the national forest. Interstate 80 cuts through the national forest past Donner Trail, Donner Pass, and the Donner Trail Memorial State Park—all reminders of the harsh winter weather here and the fated Donner Party. Many historic gold mining towns such as Truckee, Foresthill, Downieville, and Nevada City lie within or near the national forest and provide visitors with a glimpse of the early days.

More modern touches grace the national forest as well. The Pacific Crest Trail crosses the entire national forest, including Granite Chief Wilderness. This alpine area was carved by glaciers that left bald granite tops on 8,398-foot Mt. Mildred, 8,637-foot Ward Peak, and 9,006-foot Granite Chief.

The Sierra Buttes rise 8,587 feet at the north end of the national forest, the last sky-scraping Sierra rocks before the range fades into the Cascade Range. Late autumn rains paint double rainbows under the white, black, and red volcanic buttes.

The northernmost stand of giant sequoia in California lie in a canyon between two branches of the Middle Fork of the American River. A one mile, self-guided nature trail takes hikers to the Sequoia grove from the Big Trees picnic site on Mosquito Ridge Road east of Foresthill.

Kayakers and rafters run the North Fork of the American River. Part of the river has been designated a wild river and flows for more than thirty miles through deep gorges cut along the southern third of the national forest.

Dams have been built on other forks of the American River, the south and north forks of the Yuba, and the Bear River to generate power and supply water to central California. Stampede, Boca, Bullards Bar, French Meadows, Jackson Meadows, Prosser, and Lake Valley reservoirs are open to boating, fishing, waterskiing, and swimming.

All told, 78 campgrounds, 400 miles of hiking trails, 300 miles of off-road vehicle trails, and five alpine and nordic ski resorts lure enough tourists to place Tahoe National Forest among the ten most visited national forests in the nation.

In addition to those recreation activities, one-third of Tahoe National Forest is managed to harvest trees for timber, and visitors may spot logging areas from many roads. Small openings on forested slopes often indicate logging activity. Long scars usually result from avalanches, landslides, or fires.

Timber has played an important role in Plumas National Forest since its creation in 1905. Each year, Plumas produces more timber than Tahoe National Forest, and the salvaging of trees killed or damaged by the 1987 and 1988 fires may push Plumas' harvest ahead of any national forest in California for the next few years.

Loggers cut enough trees in 1987 to build almost 20,000 three-bedroom houses, a level that may be sustained through the turn of the century. Most timber trees are Jeffery, sugar, and ponderosa pine, and Douglas, red, and white fir, but not all the national forest's trees become houses. Nearly a third of California's Christmas trees—white firs—come from Plumas National Forest.

Despite all this activity, visitors may not notice timber harvesting when they drive the main highways—70, 89, and U.S. 395—that cut through or skirt the national forest. New timber sales are designed with roadside scenery in mind. Much of the logging takes place on the back side of mountains and ridges, with less-obvious logging methods such as selective cutting used on visible slopes. Logging trucks lumbering up and down the highways will remain a common sight.

Timber cuts also will be out of sight at major recreation areas such as Lakes Basin, where glaciers carved dozens of lakes in the alpine high country. Campers can stay at Grass, Jamison, Rock, Smith, and Wade lakes in the basin, but all other lakes are restricted to day uses. A network of trails links the lakes with Frazier Falls, 7,342-foot Mills Peak, and 7,812-foot Mt. Ewell.

One of Plumas National Forest's most beautiful sights is Feather Falls, located in the Feather Falls Scenic Area twenty-six miles northeast of Oroville off the Quincy-Oroville Road. The falls are reached by a two-hour, four-mile hike down and up steep, wooded slopes, but the exertion and mosquito bites are bargains in trade for the priceless majesty of the 640-foot falls, the sixth-highest in the nation. The Fall River meanders out of the Watson Basin, slips around four bends and trips over some preliminary cascades before it thunders over a barren, granite escarpment to the Middle Fork of the Feather River below.

The entire hundred-mile length of the Middle Fork of the Feather River is a wild and scenic river, starting near Beckwourth and extending to Lake Oroville. Much of the upper half is paralleled by Highway 70. Most of the final thirty-five miles before it drains into Lake Oroville is inaccessible to all but rafters, kayakers, and intrepid hikers.

The Feather and its tributaries drain the 1.4 million-acre Plumas National Forest, and the river inspired the forest's name. Hudson Bay Company trappers found Native Americans wearing blankets woven with the plumage of birds in the 1820s, and named the river to honor them. To Spanish missionaries, the waterway was Rio de las Plumas, and the name was used for the national forest.

The North Fork of the Feather River is easier to find. Witness the eight hydroelectric powerhouses scattered between Oroville and the Buck's Lake Wilderness. Highway 70 follows the river for nearly fifty miles, passing areas like Belden, where the Pacific Crest Trail crosses from the Lassen National Forest into Buck's Lake Wilderness on its fifty-mile course through Plumas National Forest.

The old Eby gold stamping mill sits by the side of the highway at Belden, its five lead pistons frozen by time in a menacing pose above a platter where ore was

V O L U N T E E R S   O N   T H E   T R A I L

Volunteers perform an increasing amount of work in budget-strapped national forests. In the Lake Tahoe Basin Management Unit, one thousand volunteers working at a clip of about ten miles a year are developing a new 150-mile trail along national forest ridges above the lake.

Men and women from across the nation come to Lake Tahoe for long weekends in the summer to clear paths, build bridges, and sing around backcountry campfires. Other volunteers are out raising money to pay the way.

The Tahoe Rim Trail Association—a non-profit group separate from the Forest Service—hopes to complete the trail so that hikers, horseback riders, and nordic skiers can make various trips through bogs, streams, meadows, and stands of red fir and Jeffery pine that surround the lake. Of course, the trail also provides spectacular views of the lake itself. To volunteer, write to Tahoe Rim Trail, P.O. Box 10156, S. Lake Tahoe, CA 95731.

crushed, then run through a mercury solution and heated. The mercury vaporized, and gold settled out. Like Eldorado and Stanislaus national forests to the south, Plumas was part of California's Mother Lode mining country.

The hope of golden riches still lures modern miners into Plumas National Forest, although many view the work more as a weekend hobby. Using metal detectors and portable floating dredges, miners scour the river bottoms for traces of the precious metal.

Somewhere on the northern fringes of Plumas National Forest—geologists can't agree where—the Sierra Nevada ends and the Cascade Range begins. That point might be where the gold stops, where milky quartz veins no longer shoot up through the granite, foreshadowing fortune. ■

The Fall River pours over a 640-foot exposed granite escarpment in Plumas National Forest to form the majestic Feather Falls. JEFF GNASS

KEEPING THE SPARKLE ON THE JEWEL

Forest watershed specialists in the Lake Tahoe Basin Management Unit take extreme measures to slow the flow of silt and pollutants from slopes and parking lots into the clear waters of Lake Tahoe.

In 1980, the Forest Service bought the lakeshore Jennings Casino site for $11.5 million. Foundations had already been laid, but national forest crews ripped out the cement and shaped the land to its original contours.

The project also moved Burke Creek out of a concrete channel that had been built to route it around the casino. In its concrete channel, the creek carried tons of silt and pollutants into Lake Tahoe. Foresters re-established the creek in its natural form,

complete with streamside vegetation and meanders. The creek's natural course allows sediments and pollutants to settle out before the water empties into the lake. Volunteers helped by planting grasses, brush, and pines. Today the resulting meadows are nesting grounds for Canada geese.

Dozens of less dramatic projects also rim the lake. Rock-lined ditches trap sediments and pollutants that run off roads. Foot-long catch basins along the low sides of hiking trails hold run-off on slopes. Thirty-year-old logging roads in Blackwood Canyon have been tilled under and replanted to stop erosion, especially on sections where off-road vehicles made illegal

forays on the closed roads.

Since 1980, national forest crews have restored more than three thousand acres of damaged slopes and streams. In addition, the Forest Service has purchased thirty thousand acres to protect certain areas from developments that would have added more pollutants to the lake. The Forest Service now owns about seventy-five percent of the land that drains into Lake Tahoe.

The work is far from over. At least two thousand acres still create serious erosion problems. National forest crews work on about one hundred to three hundred acres a year and face projects well into the next century.

TAHOE
NATIONAL FOREST DIRECTORY

POINTS OF INTEREST

DOWNIEVILLE on Hwy. 49 along the Yuba River is a restored gold-rush era village that still draws prospectors.

NORTH FORK AMERICAN RIVER is wild and scenic.

GIANT SEQUOIA northern-most grove in California is west of Foresthill, between Mosquito Ridge Rd. and North Fork American River.

RECREATIONAL ACTIVITIES

HIKING AND RIDING More than 600 miles of trails open to hikers, horseback riders, and mountain bicyclists.

CAMPING Restricted to designated sites along Yuba River and some lakes in Tahoe Forest and rest of national forest open. Forest Service maintains 99 campgrounds in the national forest. Contact district ranger stations for fee and reservation information.

PICNICKING Allowed throughout the national forest and at one of 38 designated day-use spots in the national forest and at the lake.

ALPINE SKIING Alpine Meadows (13 lifts); Boreal (9 lifts); Donner Ski Ranch (4 lifts); Granlibakken (2 lifts/tows); Soda Springs (3 lifts); Squaw Valley (26 lifts/tows, 2 trams); Sugar Bowl (8 lifts, 1 tram); Tahoe Donner (3 lifts/tows); Tahoe Ski Bowl (5 lifts/tows); and Northstar-at-Tahoe (10 lifts/tows, 1 tram).

CROSS-COUNTRY SKIING Allowed on many national forest backcountry roads; larger alpine resorts also maintain nordic trails.

SCENIC DRIVES Highway 49 follows the Yuba River under the menacing Sierra Buttes and into Mother Lode country.

HUNTING California Fish & Game license required. Seasons on mule deer, black bear, squirrel, cottontail rabbit, blue grouse, bandtail pigeon, mourning dove, mountain quail, ducks, and geese.

FISHING California Fish & Game license required. American, Yuba, and Truckee rivers contain wild and stocked trout.

OFF-ROAD VEHICLES AND SNOWMOBILES Green stickers and spark arrestors required. Allowed on most national forest backcountry roads and some trails.

ADMINISTRATIVE OFFICES

TAHOE FOREST HEADQUARTERS Highway 49 & Coyote St., Nevada City, CA 95959 (916) 265-4531

NEVADA CITY RANGER DISTRICT Highway 49 & Coyote St., Nevada City, CA 95959 (916) 265-4538

FORESTHILL RANGER DISTRICT 22830 Foresthill Road, Foresthill CA 95631 (916) 367-2224

DOWNIEVILLE RANGER DISTRICT 15924 Hwy. 49, Box 1, Camptonville CA 95922 (916) 288-3231

SIERRAVILLE RANGER DISTRICT P.O. Box 95, Sierraville CA 96126 (916) 994-3401

TRUCKEE RANGER DISTRICT P.O. Box 399, Truckee CA 95734 (916) 587-3558

LAKE TAHOE BASIN
MANAGEMENT UNIT DIRECTORY

P O I N T S   O F   I N T E R E S T

LAKE TAHOE VISITOR CENTER on the north end of the Pope-Baldwin Recreation Area has free brochures, gives guided tours, and is surrounded by self-guided nature walks. Nearby stream profile chamber has underground viewing area with explanations of trout and kokanee salmon.

R E C R E A T I O N   A R E A

POPE-BALDWIN Complex on west shore of Lake Tahoe. Visitor center, two beaches, two campgrounds, trailer lot, picnic ground, horse stables, bicycle path, cabin rentals, boat rentals, resort, boat ramp. Historic Tallac mansion buildings.

R E C R E A T I O N A L   A C T I V I T I E S

HIKING AND RIDING Pacific Crest Trail covers 70 miles from the Sierra Buttes to Desolation Wilderness. Volunteers cut about 10 new miles a year of a planned trail on the ridges circling Lake Tahoe.

CAMPING Four designated spots on Lake Tahoe shore.

ALPINE SKIING Heavenly Valley (19 lifts/tows, 1 tram); Homewood (7 lifts/tows); Incline (7 lifts).

CROSS-COUNTRY SKIING Groomed or marked trails at these Lake Tahoe sites: Tahoe Meadows (east); Spooner Lake (east); Pope-Baldwin (south); Angora Lookout (south); Trout Creek (south); Echo Lakes (south); Benwood Meadows (south); Big Meadow (south); Grass Lake (south); Hope Valley (south); Paige Meadows (west); Blackwood Canyon (west); Sugar Pine Point State Park (west); Meeks Creek (west); and McKinney (west).

SCENIC DRIVES Two-hour tour around Lake Tahoe, on routes 89, 28, and 50. Forest Service cassette tape narrates history and explains highlights such as the Tallac Cross and Meeks Bay.

FISHING Rainbow, golden, brook trout, and kokanee salmon in Lake Tahoe and its tributaries. Nevada or California license required to fish Lake Tahoe.

OFF-ROAD VEHICLES AND SNOWMOBILES Green stickers and spark arrestors required. At least 10 designated routes on Lake Tahoe shores for both ORVs and snowmobiles.

A D M I N I S T R A T I V E   O F F I C E S

LAKE TAHOE BASIN HEADQUARTERS P.O. Box 731002, 870 Emerald Bay Rd., S. Lake Tahoe, CA 95731 (916) 573-2600

LAKE TAHOE VISITOR CENTER (summers only) S. Lake Tahoe, CA (916) 573-2674

PLUMAS
NATIONAL FOREST DIRECTORY

P O I N T S   O F   I N T E R E S T

FEATHER FALLS at 640 feet is the sixth-highest waterfall in the United States. Reached by 4-mile trail off Rd. 27262, northwest of Oroville.

MIDDLE FORK FEATHER RIVER is a Wild & Scenic River. Motorized vehicles are generally banned within a quarter-mile of shore. Rated rated Class VI (expert) for white water rafting in the spring and hike-in anglers in the summer and fall.

R E C R E A T I O N   A R E A S

BUCKS LAKE Four campgrounds, two resorts, Bucks Lake observation site, Mill Creek Trail, and trailheads to Pacific Crest Trail. Fishing on Bucks Lake. On county road 414, west of Quincy.

LAKES BASIN One campground, one picnic ground, and dozens of small glacial cirques with jagged granite peaks for backdrops. A network of hiking and equestrian trails link the lakes and other destinations such as Mills Peak Lookout, Red Fir Nature Trail, and Frazier Falls. Hunting and fishing are permitted in the area. On county road 519 and 721 in the southwest corner of the national forest.

LAKE DAVIS Camping restricted to 3 campgrounds; 4 boat launches, hiking trails. Fishing on the lake. Smith Peak Lookout 7 miles southwest of the lake. Off-road vehicles banned, but snowmobiles allowed. On county roads 112 and 126, north of Portola.

R E C R E A T I O N A L   A C T I V I T I E S

HIKING AND RIDING 341 miles of trails, including 70 miles of the Pacific Crest Trail, open to hikers, horseback riders, and mountain bicyclists. Two National Recreation Trails: Feather Falls, which leads to the falls; and Hartman Bar, which drops 2,000 feet from Hartman Bar Ridge to the Middle Fork Feather River.

CAMPING Allowed throughout the national forest and at 38 campgrounds maintained by the Forest Service. Check with forest offices for fee and reservation information.

ALPINE SKIING Two poma lifts and one rope tow at Plumas-Eureka State Park, which is within the national forest, on county road 507 west of Mohawk.

CROSS-COUNTRY SKIING Allowed on most backcountry national forest service roads; some groomed trails at Plumas-Eureka State Park.

SCENIC DRIVES Hwy. 70 snakes north from Oroville along the North Fork Feather River until the road joins Hwy. 89. On the way, the road winds through pine and fir forests, logging operations, an old gold ore stamp at Belden, and dams and power stations that trap the river water to generate electricity and drinking water for Central and Southern California.

HUNTING California Fish & Game license required. Prohibited in some recreation areas and state game refuge. Seasons on blacktail and mule deer, black bear, small game, upland birds, and waterfowl.

FISHING California Fish & Game license required. More than 175 lakes and 950 miles of rivers and streams, many stocked with rainbow trout. Park in day use lots at the recreation areas, or in campgrounds.

OFF-ROAD VEHICLES AND SNOWMOBILES Green stickers and spark arrestors required. Allowed on many national forest backcountry roads, except on some posted roads at Bucks Lake. Banned in wilderness. Groomed snowmobile routes at Bucks Lake and on Gold Lake Hwy.

A D M I N I S T R A T I V E   O F F I C E S

FOREST HEADQUARTERS 159 Lawrence St., Quincy CA 95971 (916) 283-2050

BECKWORTH RANGER DISTRICT P.O. Box 7, Blairsden CA 96103 (916) 836-2575

GREENVILLE RANGER DISTRICT P.O. Box 329, Greenville CA 95947 (916) 284-7126

LA PORTE RANGER DISTRICT P.O. Drawer 369, Challenge CA 95925 (916) 675-2462

OROVILLE RANGER DISTRICT 875 Mitchell Ave., Oroville CA 95965 (916) 534-6500

MILFORD RANGER DISTRICT Milford CA 96121 (916) 253-2223

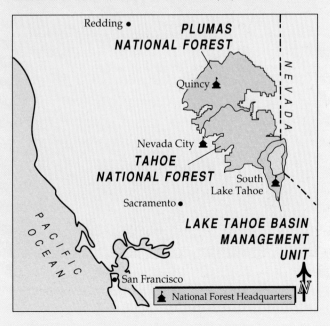

The South Warner Wilderness in the Modoc National Forest is one of the most remote and unspoiled spots in California. Warren Peak rises behind Patterson Lake. DAVID MUENCH

Modoc and Lassen

*Lonely
lands with
a fiery past*

For fifteen million years, the earth spewed molten lava across most of northeastern California, creating the long plateaus, jumbled lava beds, and volcanic mountains of Modoc and Lassen national forests.

These are forgotten forests, overlooked by wilderness trekkers and casual tourists. Locals know the fishing is incomparable, the scenery spectacular, and the geography telling, but they are often left alone to explore the land and its abundant wildlife.

These are also working forests. About 55,000 cattle and sheep graze on the two national forests, and loggers cut enough ponderosa pine from these lands to build more than 12,000 three-bedroom houses a year.

In another type of home building, wildlife biologists have built hundreds of small islands and dug hundreds more shallow ponds in meadows and intermittent lake beds on both national forests to create nesting areas for ducks and geese. The areas are big hits—as many as three pairs of geese have nested together on one island—and foresters plan to build hundreds more.

Human history has been less harmonious. Native Americans lived here for centuries before fur trappers from the Hudson Bay Company wandered into the area in the 1820s. The trappers soon left, but American settlers began drifting in from the east and north. Their arrival touched off decades of conflict with the Modoc Indians, ending with the bloody Modoc War.

Modoc National Forest contains diverse landscapes. Much of its 1.9 million acres lies on the Modoc Plateau, a high, cold desert as removed from California's typical pine- and fir-covered national forests as the low chaparral desert of the Cleveland National Forest more than seven hundred miles south.

Yet the Warner Mountains that form the eastern flank of Modoc National Forest have steep, rugged slopes of ponderosa and Jeffery pine that resemble slopes in the Sierra Nevada, and the national forest's western flank near the Shasta-Trinity National Forest contains moist stands of mixed conifers.

Nonetheless, the long, spartan Modoc Plateau dominates Modoc National Forest. The plateau formed about thirty million years ago when molten lava seeped up along block faults. The black basalt lava filled a valley that once served as the junction of the Sierra Nevada and Klamath Mountains.

Purple sagebrush, rabbitbrush, and snowbrush grew on the thin mantle of dirt that eventually covered the plateau. Now the area is called Devil's Garden and supports a 300,000-acre forest of western juniper, the largest juniper stand in the national forest system. The trees are felled for fence posts and firewood.

About fifteen million years ago, a second, shiny layer of basalt bubbled up through vents and formed razor-sharp obsidian. These eruptions left 10- and 20-square mile piles of lava, such as Glass Mountain and the Burnt Lava Flow. Glass Mountain's last known eruption was only three hundred years ago, and it still belches stinky, sulfurous gases from vents.

Burnt Lava Flow and Glass Mountain lie on the western side of Modoc National Forest, south of Lava Beds National Monument. Cinder roads skirt the lips of both features. The menacing black piles rise ten feet above the road on one side while pine and fir forests grow on the other side. Nearby Medicine Lake is a filled volcanic crater with picnic sites on the shore.

Most of the valleys and meadows in the Modoc area once were covered by fields of waving, waist-high grasses, but between 1870 and 1900 livestock so overgrazed the land that much of it was reduced to dust beds. By 1903, cattlemen petitioned President Theodore Roosevelt to create a forest reserve and limit sheep grazing. Roosevelt fashioned two reserves in 1904—Warner Mountains and Modoc—that were combined in 1908 to form Modoc National Forest. The new status protected the lands from wasteful timber practices and overgrazing, and productivity gradually was restored. Today, 1.3 million acres of the 1.9-million-acre national forest are carefully managed as grazing land.

This land also supports mule deer, pronghorn antelope, and wild horses. Fairchild Swamp is a good place to catch a glimpse of the wild horses, living reminders of Modoc National Forest's earlier days.

A VIOLENT WAR FOR A VIOLENT LAND

When Modoc Indians saw Hudson Bay Company trappers coming over the Klamath Mountains to their Tule Lake and Clear Lake territory, they assumed the worst. Leaders prophesied the traders were only the first wave of a tide that would sweep over and destroy a way of life that revolved around the manufacture and trade of buckskins, furs, and rabbitskin blankets.

Known to other Indians as fiercely aggressive, the Modoc vowed to fight the invaders to the death. They fought and they

died, but not before decades of skirmishes and covert operations wiped out many white and Modoc families.

Ranchers waged bloody campaigns through the 1850s and 1860s. A settler named Ben Wright was so vengeful he schemed to gain the trust of a Modoc village. That accomplished, he set up an elaborate peace feast where a band of vigilantes waited in the woods. On Wright's signal, they massacred the Modoc.

The bloodflow ebbed until the Modoc War of 1872-73. Kentipoos, a Modoc known to settlers as Captain Jack, led a band of fifty-seven warriors in a guerrilla war fought from the lava caves in what is now Lava Beds National Monument.

Kentipoos, whose father had been killed by Wright's party, raided settlers' munitions and food supplies, killing a dozen settlers in the process. The war ended on October 3, 1873, when Kentipoos and three warriors were hanged.

Vestages of California's Wild West past, about 350 wild horses, right, roam chaparral- and juniper-covered Modoc Plateau.
ROGER & DONNA AITKENHEAD

Tule Lake, left, on the northern border of the Modoc National Forest is a national wildlife refuge. The lake and its shores harbor thousands of migratory ducks and geese. Wildlife biologists estimate that at least eighty-five percent of the state's waterfowl habitat has been drained and developed, making this site even more precious.
ROBERT McKENZIE

Lassen National Forest is marked by lava flows, ice caves, and lovely mountain lakes. Located between Redding and Susanville at the juncture of the Sierra Nevada and the Cascade Range, this national forest delights visitors with abundant wildlife, good fishing, and widespread evidence of past volcanic activity.

Some of the volcanic activity is relatively recent. In 1915, 10,457-foot Lassen Peak completed a year of minor eruptions with an astonishing explosion that sent steam and rock fragments 25,000 feet into the sky. Rumblings continued for another year, and in 1916 the peak and the area immediately around it were transferred from the Forest Service to the National Park Service as Lassen Volcanic National Park. Lassen National Forest's 1.2 million acres completely surround the 106,000-acre national park.

Despite the loss of Lassen Peak, Lassen National Forest still contains a wealth of volcanic features. Ancient lava flows often made caves as they swept through both Lassen and Modoc national forests. Many of the caves now contain permanent ice. Although most ice caves are too small to explore, Brockman Flats Cave in Lassen National Forest attracts experienced spelunkers who rappel 120 feet into the sunken cave mouth to explore lava rooms covered by four-foot sheets of ice.

The national forest's Subway Cave makes an easier

More than 130 miles of the 2,620-mile Pacific Crest Trail, top right, winds through Lassen National Forest, crossing the Feather River Canyon, Lassen Volcanic National Park, and the dry Hat Creek Rim. BILL HEAD

Hat Creek, right, cuts through a 25-mile-long plateau of hardened rock created by a lava flow 2,000 years ago. The snowcapped volcano— incorporated into a national park after its eruption—rises in the background. LARRY BURTON

tour. Red reflectors mark five interpretive signs on the hike through a 1,300-foot lava tube, past Stubtoe Hall, Lucifer's Cul-de-sac, The Sanctum, and Lavacicle Lane. The tube formed as the surface of a lava flow cooled while hot magma continued to flow inside the hardened shell. The flow left pumice on the floor at Stubtoe and dripping pendants that formed lavacicles on the ceiling. Bring a flashlight or a lantern.

Nearby Spattercone Trail takes visitors on a 1.5-mile hike past stands of ponderosa and Jeffrey pine, volcanic craters, lava domes, and collapsed lava tubes. A free brochure at the trailhead explains all the features at fifteen viewpoints along the trail.

The lava landscape is so porous that water percolates through it quickly, leaving few creeks. But to twist Newtonian physics, what goes down must come up, and Lassen National Forest contains several lakes, including

spring-fed Crater Lake in the shadows of 7,420-foot Crater Mountain. The lake is full year-round with water and stocked trout. Motorboats are banned, but a small campground overlooks golden quaking aspen, whose shimmering reflection is diffused by early morning mists that float above the lake on crisp autumn days.

Nearby Eagle Lake is busier. Come fall, deer and upland bird hunters inhabit the lakeside campgrounds, which have 325 campsites and a group campground. In the spring, osprey nest on the north shore. The gusty lake is a snag-free haven for sailors and waterskiers. In the spring of 1989 it became a safe harbor for terminally ill and developmentally disabled children who camp at a special $2 million complex sponsored by Lassen National Forest, Eagle Lake Childrens Charity, and Northern California Golden Arches Association.

Once lowered for irrigation, Eagle Lake is slowly rising

The neck of a golden eagle, right, bulges with half-swallowed prey. The raptor engages in a rambunctious mating flight that is occasionally fatal for novices who collide with potential mates at high speed in midair. JEFF FOOTT

Lassen National Forest's rich growth of pines makes it one of the most productive timbering areas in California, below left. RON SANFORD

Least chipmunks, below right, are not among the nine threatened and endangered species inhabiting the Lassen National Forest, but they are prey for the endangered bald eagle and peregrine falcon, and the spotted owl and great gray owl. BILL HEAD

to its historic level. The lake is fed by several creeks but has no natural outlet, so as lake water evaporates, minerals and nutrients stay behind. The resulting alkaline-rich environment contains the unique Eagle Lake trout, a species adapted to the alkaline water. The trout were thought to have become extinct by 1950 when the lake was lowered for irrigation. However, a few trout were found hovering in Pine Creek, one of the lake's tributaries, and the state established a fishery that today harvests roe, raises fingerlings, and plants thousands of young trout in surrounding lakes. Other fish also inhabit the national forest. Deer, Mill, and Antelope creeks are the farthest inland spawning grounds in California for ocean-going salmon and steelhead trout.

Fertile lands north and west of the lakes are lined with acres of ponderosa pines and white firs that help make Lassen one of California's most efficient timber-producing national forests. Loggers here annually cut 5- and 20-acre patches of second-growth pines.

In addition, Lassen National Forest contains three wilderness areas. Ishi Wilderness contains the land where a Native American called Ishi hid from ranchers until 1911. Caribou Wilderness is a land of high lakes—but no caribou. Thousand Lakes Wilderness is marked by dramatic cliffs and buttes—but far fewer than a thousand lakes.

The wilderness areas receive relatively few visitors. They remain—much like the rest of both Lassen and Modoc national forests—little-known places of beauty and wonder in a strange and beautiful land. ■

A WILDERNESS FOR ISHI

No one knew quite what to make of Ishi, the Yahi Indian who in 1911 wandered out of the wilderness around Black Rock in Lassen National Forest.

Ishi's ancestors were Yana and Yahi Indians who were exterminated by ranchers and settlers in the 1860s. Part of the problem was an unfortunate clash of cultural values. The Yahi were hunter-gatherers who had no concept of domestic herds. As a result, they routinely killed dim-witted cattle, much to the undying fury of ranchers.

By 1870, the ranchers presumed their task of eradication was complete. Instead, a small group of Indians went into hiding in

the remote, rugged lands behind Indian Ridge and remained out of sight for nearly forty years.

Utility company surveyors marking maps for a possible dam and powerhouse stumbled on a small Yahi camp in 1908. They found an old woman—Ishi's mother—and a hot fire. They plundered the camp, leaving the woman alone. Ishi, his uncle, and a female cousin fled the camp moments before, but they went in separate directions. Ishi returned to the camp and moved his mother. He never saw the others again.

Ishi's mother died quickly, and Ishi lived alone for three years before surrendering to

startled settlers near Mill Creek.

When he walked out of the woods, Ishi was whisked to jail. No local Indians could understand Ishi's dialect. Finally, a professor at the University of California—Berkeley heard the tale, and he and Ishi could converse well enough to understand one another.

Ishi lived the last four years of his life in the basement of a Berkeley museum, working as a janitor. The man who said he never recalled an illness died in 1915 of tuberculosis. In 1984 Congress dedicated 40,670 acres of his hideaway in Lassen National Forest as the Ishi Wilderness.

MODOC
NATIONAL FOREST DIRECTORY

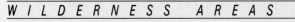

POINTS OF INTEREST

BURNT LAVA FLOW, MEDICINE LAKE GLASS FLOW, and **GLASS MOUNTAIN GLASS FLOW** are miles of lava and obsidian squeezed into old-growth pine and fir forests. All three areas are located on the west side of the national forest, south of Lava Beds National Monument, on national forest roads 49 and 97.

DEVIL'S GARDEN is part of the long, flat Modoc Plateau. The grass- and western juniper-covered plain is range land for cattle and sheep, as well as antelope, mule deer, and wild horses. Take national forest road 46 north from Hwy. 139, north of Canby.

WILDERNESS AREAS

SOUTH WARNER 70,000 acres of sage- and juniper-covered lowlands, topped by alpine

high country of white fir, glacial lakes, and quaking aspen. Best travel time is mid-July to October. Almost 80 miles of trails lace the area.

RECREATIONAL ACTIVITIES

HIKING AND RIDING Two national recreation trails—Blue Lake in the South Warner Mtns. and Highgrade in the North Warners—are among 118 miles of trails open to hikers, horseback riders, and mountain bicyclists.

CAMPING Allowed throughout the national forest and at 20 campgrounds maintained by the Forest Service.

PICNICKING Allowed throughout the national forest.

ALPINE SKIING Cedar Pass Ski Hill. A small slope with one T-bar and one rope-tow, run by a local club in the South Warner Mountains.

SCENIC DRIVES Forest road 46, north of Canby, passes through miles of rabbitbrush- and western juniper-covered plains in Devil's Garden Research Natural Area. Forest roads 97 and 46 lead to Glass Mountain and Burnt Lava Flow between fir and pine forests on one side and volcanic features on the other side.

HUNTING California Fish & Game license required. Seasons on mule deer, pronghorn antelope, tree squirrels, mourning dove, blue grouse, waterfowl, and small game.

FISHING California Fish & Game license required. Reservoirs, streams, and lakes stocked with rainbow trout; Little Medicine Lake stocked with arctic grayling.

OFF-ROAD VEHICLES Green stickers and spark arrestors required. No designated trails or staging areas; allowed throughout the national forest, except in wilderness and Devil's Garden Research Natural Area.

A D M I N I S T R A T I V E   O F F I C E S

FOREST HEADQUARTERS 441 N. Main St., Alturas CA 96101 (916) 233-5811

BIG VALLEY RANGER DISTRICT P.O. Box 159, Adin CA 96006 (916) 299-3215

DEVILS GARDEN RANGER DISTRICT P.O. Box 5, Canby CA 96015 (916) 233-4611

DOUBLEHEAD RANGER DISTRICT P.O. Box 818, Tulelake CA 96134 (916) 667-2247

WARNER MOUNTAIN RANGER DISTRICT P.O. Box 220, Cedarville CA 96104 (916) 279-6116

LASSEN
NATIONAL FOREST DIRECTORY

P O I N T S   O F   I N T E R E S T

SUBWAY CAVE on Hwy. 89 in Hat Creek Valley is a 1/3-mile, self-guided hike through lava tube. Bring a flashlight to avoid obstacles and read signs and a jacket to stay warm, even in summer.

LASSEN PEAK is contained in Lassen Volcanic National Park but is visible from the surrounding national forest. The park actually was carved from the national forest after the 10,457-foot volcanic peak erupted in 1915.

R E C R E A T I O N   A R E A S

EAGLE LAKE Six campgrounds, four boat ramps, a marina, beaches, a picnic ground, and an amphitheater where nature programs are presented on summer evenings. Wildlife sanctuary on northwest shore is off-limits to humans but home to osprey, bald eagles, white pelicans, and pronghorn antelope. North of Susanville on Lassen County road A-1.

HAT CREEK Six campgrounds, four picnic grounds, Subway Cave, Deer Hollow, and Spatter Cone self-guided nature trails, and trailhead to Pacific Crest Trail centered around intersection of Hwys. 44 and 89. Hat Creek Rim is elevated lava plateau that looks over valley where lava flowed but did not settle.

LAKE ALMANOR Five campgrounds, three picnic grounds, two boat ramps, and a beach on west shore of lake created in 1914 when Pacific Gas & Electric Co. dammed the Feather River. On Hwys. 89 and 147, southwest of Susanville.

SILVER LAKE Two campgrounds, two picnic grounds, and hiking trails that link nine small lakes, at junction of county roads 10 and 110, east of Caribou Wilderness.

W I L D E R N E S S   A R E A S

CARIBOU 20,000 acres just east of Lassen Volcanic National Park with lakes and cinder cones on a wooded, rolling plateau. Named for Caribou Peaks.

ISHI 42,000 acres named for a man believed to be the last Native American to surrender to white culture, in 1911. Pine forests in the high elevations and Mill and Deer creeks dominate the area.

THOUSAND LAKES 16,000 acres of lava and granite domes, stands of lodgepole pine, meadows, bare plains above timberline, and many lakes.

R E C R E A T I O N A L   A C T I V I T I E S

HIKING AND RIDING Almost 350 miles of trails, including 120 miles of the Pacific Crest Trail, open to hikers, horseback riders, and mountain bicyclists. Bizz Johnson Trail follows old rail line for 25 miles along the rugged Susan River Canyon.

CAMPING Allowed throughout the national forest and at 46 campgrounds maintained by Forest Service. Check with district rangers for fee and reservation information.

PICNICKING Allowed throughout the national forest and at designated spots in recreation areas.

ALPINE SKIING Two small resorts operate with one lift and one rope tow each: Coppervale, south of Susanville on Hwy. 36; and Stover Mtn. on Hwy. 36 west of Lake Almanor.

CROSS-COUNTRY SKIING Ungroomed trails on many Forest Service backcountry roads and the Bizz Johnson Trail. Some groomed trails at Eskimo Hill, on Hwy. 44 west of Lassen Volcanic National Park, and McGowan Lake, on Hwy. 89 near Mineral.

SCENIC DRIVES Hwy. 44 north and west from Susanville to its junction with Hwy. 89 passes through meadows where cattle and sheep graze in the summer and geese and ducks nest in the spring, slopes covered in Douglas fir, and logging sites. At the 44-89 junction, the road heads south and west along the Hat Creek Rim and through more wooded slopes. Hwy. 32 from Chico to Hwy. 36 passes through pine, fir, and cedar forests and hugs Deer Creek.

HUNTING California Fish & Game license required. Seasons on mule and blacktail deer, black bear, pronghorn antelope, red fox, and waterfowl species and upland birds.

FISHING California Fish & Game license required. More than 500 miles of fishable streams and 3,000 acres of lakes with native and stocked rainbow and brown trout. Eagle Lake trout unique to Eagle Lake.

OFF-ROAD VEHICLES AND SNOWMOBILES Green stickers and spark arrestors required. Forest Service backcountry roads open to four-wheel drives in summer and most are open to snowmobiles in winter. Ashpan on Hwy. 44 west of Lassen Volcanic National Park, and Morgan Summit on Hwy. 36 east of Mineral, have marked and groomed snowmobile trails.

A D M I N I S T R A T I V E   O F F I C E S

FOREST HEADQUARTERS 55 S. Sacramento St., Susanville CA 96130 (916) 257-2151

ALMANOR RANGER DISTRICT P.O. Box 767, Chester CA 96020 (916) 258-2141

EAGLE LAKE RANGER DISTRICT 55 S. Sacramento St., Susanville CA 96130 (916) 257-2595

HAT CREEK RANGER DISTRICT P.O. Box 220, Fall River Mills CA 96028 (916) 336-5521

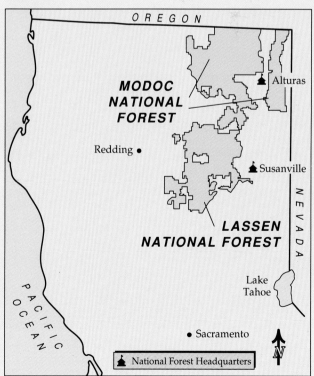

A May sun rises over some of the thousands of fingers and coves created when the Bureau of Reclamation completed Shasta Dam in 1945. When full, as it usually is in May, Shasta Lake has 370 miles of shoreline, more than San Francisco Bay. JEFF GNASS

SHASTA-TRINITY

The largest of all

Mt. Shasta rises 14,162 feet above sea level to dominate the Shasta-Trinity National Forest in northern California. Though not the highest peak in California, Mt. Shasta is the most massive—a giant jumble of ancient volcanoes melded together on a base seventeen miles across.

California's largest mountain fits nicely in California's largest national forest, itself a giant formed by merging separate entities. Shasta National Forest was created in 1905, Trinity National Forest in 1907. In 1954 the two adjacent national forests were combined into one administrative unit, creating a 2.1-million-acre national forest unit that wraps around the head of the Sacramento Valley for more than 130 miles.

Shasta-Trinity's size provides room for a wide array of recreation and resource activities. Perhaps more completely than other national forests in California, Shasta-Trinity illustrates the balance between development and preservation that Gifford Pinchot, the first Forest Service chief, sought for all national forests in the early 1900s.

In addition to Mt. Shasta, the Shasta-Trinity National Forest contains two other popular landmarks—Shasta Lake and Clair Engle Lake (also called Trinity Lake). These reservoirs were created by the Bureau of Reclamation to control floods on the McCloud, Pit, Squaw, Trinity, and Sacramento rivers and provide water for irrigation, power generation, and domestic and industrial use in the Sacramento Valley and San Francisco Bay area.

Logging, grazing, and mining also take place in Shasta-Trinity National Forest. Timber sales each year produce enough ponderosa pine and Douglas fir to build 22,000 three-bedroom houses. Meadows provide grazing land for more than five thousand cattle and sheep. Gold miners still work claims in the national forest's mountains and streams.

Obviously Shasta-Trinity is a working national forest, but thousands of visitors enjoy it as an immense playground. From Little Glass Mountain and McCloud River on the east, Mt. Shasta and Shasta Lake in the middle, to a wild and scenic river and Yolla Bolly-Middle Eel Wilderness on the south, Shasta-Trinity National Forest contains an astonishing array of scenic beauty and outdoor recreation opportunities.

Volcanic craters and ancient lava flows roll into Shasta-Trinity from Modoc National Forest on the northeast. Thirty miles west, Mt. Shasta rises above Hemlock and Fisk Ridges where old cedars tower over second-growth stands of Jeffery and sugar pine. Hundred-foot-tall cedars also line Highway 89 on the drive to Shasta, forming a canopied promenade broken by fleeting glimpses of stark, mottled glaciers atop the alabaster mountain.

Highway 89 follows McCloud River past three campgrounds and a picnic area. The lower McCloud is a wild trout stream where fishing is restricted to single barbless hooks. The river contains California's only population of bull trout—also called Dolly Varden—

The north face of Mt. Shasta, right—really the mass of four volcanoes melded together—glows above brilliant quaking aspen. ROBERT McKENZIE

Llamas are appearing more frequently on pack trails in California's national forests, bottom left. The animals are popular with many outfitters for their equanimity and climbing ability. DEBBY COOPER

An early frost sugar-coats wild strawberries, bottom right. The saw-toothed leaves stay deep green until winter, when they turn bright red. The berries ripen in the fall. The delicate, white flowers bloom in spring. LINDA J. MOORE

Serviceberry and red buds flower along the Trinity River in the Shasta-Trinity National Forest. Blossoming in spring, they add colorful detail to the forest canopy.   WILLARD CLAY

and any caught must be released. The river also offers excellent fishing for brown and rainbow trout. Long meadows along the river attract cross-country skiers in the winter.

Mt. Shasta rises as the most prominent peak in northern California. According to an old saying, Mt. Shasta's majestic beauty is inspiring from every angle except one—atop its summit. When you stand on it, you can't see its graceful form.

Different scenic views are found on the historic Sisson-Callahan Trail. Hikers on this national recreation trail encounter meadow wildflowers blooming yellow and red in the spring and summer, tranquil Deadfall Lakes, and 9,025-foot Mt. Eddy. First cut by game animals and later trod by Indians, cattlemen, and miners, the trail follows the North Fork Sacramento River and climbs from 3,500 feet at Lake Siskiyou to 8,020 feet at Deadfall Summit.

Yet another trail—the Pacific Crest Trail—traverses 154 miles of the Shasta-Trinity backcountry, passing through two of the national forest's five wilderness areas. Mt. Shasta Wilderness, with its bevy of climbers, hikers, campers, and cross-country skiers, is the most used. The massive Trinity Alps and smaller Castle Crags, Chanchelulla, and Yolla Bolly-Middle Eel wildernesses are more remote.

Castle Crags Wilderness lies just below The Eddys range, just above Castle Crags State Park, and wraps around the sheer, 6,000-foot granite cliffs and spires of Castle Crags. The Pacific Crest Trail lies in the morning shadows cast by the jagged crags, and a 55-mile auto tour loops around the wilderness from Lake Siskiyou.

Almost due west from Castle Crags at the head of

Ski mountaineering in the Mt. Shasta Wilderness and nordic touring in the meadows below the wilderness boundary are popular pastimes, above. A ski area is planned for the south face in the 1990s. ROBERT McKENZIE

The snow-capped summit of Mt. Shasta is covered by glaciers and alluring but treacherous ice caves.
DAVID CAVAGNARO

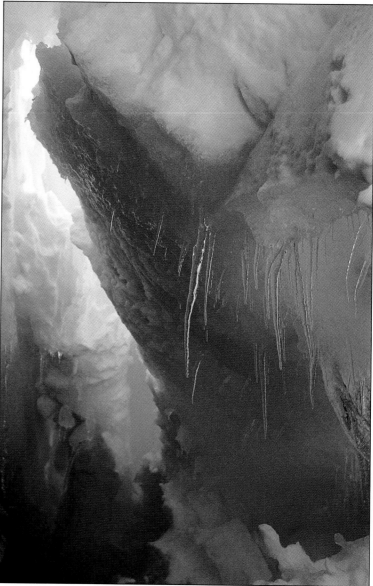

Trinity Lake, Coffee Creek Road twists and climbs seven miles along private land surrounded by the vast Trinity Alps Wilderness. The road is a wonderful tour for those who can't hike the high country. It ends at Big Flat, where operators of two small resorts greet patrons eager for quiet and backcountry trekkers anxious for wilderness adventure.

Coffee Creek Ranger Station at the beginning of the road offers a spectacular look up into the Trinity Alps Wilderness—and back into time. Civilian Conservation Corps crews built the station in the 1930s by following standard drawings for ranger stations throughout the state. Ranchers settled the creek in the mid-1800s, and cattle still graze meadows along the road.

Foresters are restoring the nearby Bowerman Barn, a cavernous structure built sometime after 1860 out of three- and four-foot wide planks from logging flumes. Constructed with sturdy pegs and nails, the barn stands fifty-five feet high with a double-deck hayloft and a basement for stock corrals.

Coffee Creek may have come by its colorful name from a perhaps apocryphal tale of a load of beans that spilled into the waterway. It seems more likely that muddy spring run-offs are responsible.

At times the creek becomes more than just muddy. A 1964 landslide rolled through from Battle Creek, slinging five acres of hillside, trees, and rocks ahead of it and changing the course of both creeks. The area is still unstable and may come loose again someday.

Part of the Trinity Alps Wilderness was originally set aside by Congress as a primitive area in 1932 and received wilderness designation in 1984. The wilderness

A pygmy owl peers from the hollow of a dead but still-standing tree, left. Foresters call these trees "snags" and often require loggers to leave them standing for use by birds, rodents, and insects. WILLIAM LLOYD

High in the wilderness, a man and his best friend pause to rest, above. Foresters urge hikers to leave dogs at home unless the animals are well-trained. RON SANFORD

spreads over 513,100 acres in three national forests—Shasta-Trinity, Klamath, and Six Rivers. Its barren granite peaks, rough moraines, and eighty-one high country lakes were carved by four waves of glaciers. Lush meadows filled with alpine flowers soften the area's rugged beauty.

Trinity Alps has long been a popular wilderness. Horseback riders gather at trailheads along the North Fork of the Trinity River during the fall hunting seasons, and hikers frequent trailheads in the Canyon Creek area. Foresters can help hikers select trails that range from easy to expert, popular to ignored.

Other forest visitors prefer water trails. Shasta and Clair Engle lakes cover almost 50,000 acres and attract two million houseboaters, swimmers, and anglers. Many come early each summer to escape the sweltering heat of Sacramento Valley. More than fifty public campgrounds surround the lakes, including eight campgrounds reached only by boat. The campgrounds are especially busy from Memorial Day through the Fourth of July, and again around Labor Day.

Resorts, marinas, motels, and boat ramps rim Shasta Lake, where on summer and holiday weekends as many as 1,750 boats a day roll off trailers and splash into the water, carrying forty thousand people to cooler comfort than the land can offer. Foresters calculate the lake can safely handle up to two thousand boats a day and are planning for the future when permits or quotas may be necessary.

Houseboats are the craft of choice on Shasta Lake. Families from the San Francisco Bay area have

Ferns and mountain dogwoods nudge onto Canyon Creek Trail, below, in the Trinity Alps Wilderness. The 513,100-acre wilderness covers parts of the Shasta-Trinity, Klamath, and Six Rivers national forests. LARRY ULRICH

Rock strata, right, give Sawtooth Ridge in the Trinity Alps Wilderness its name. Glaciers carved the distinctive rock. DAVID MUENCH

established generations-long traditions of point-to-point lake touring by houseboat. The order may change, but almost eighty percent of all houseboaters spend a day at Shasta Dam on the south end of the lake, then move west to the old copper mine sites for a day, then spend a third day at Squaw Creek, a narrow, limestone canyon. Day four is spent touring the McCloud River arm of the lake, and day five—for the courageous—is a tour of Pit River arm, which is studded with barely submerged trees.

Many boaters swap the Pit River excursion for a one-hour tour of Shasta Caverns. Landlubbers can reach the largest developed cave system in California from a tour boat that plies Shasta Lake's McCloud River arm near Bailey Cove. To tour the privately owned caverns, with names like Dome Room, Discovery Room, and Crystal Room, is to travel back in times when weather and geology combined to form stalactites, stalagmites, and hundreds of magnificently detailed formations. The caves are damp and cool—and the forces of nature are still at work creating new limestone sculptures.

Visitors also flock to the Whiskeytown-Shasta-Trinity National Recreation Area that includes all three lakes. The area was created in 1965 after the Bureau of Reclamation finished its dam projects and turned 203,587 acres of canyons, meadows, and newly created lakeshores over to the National Park Service and Forest Service. Park rangers manage the lands around Whiskeytown Lake. Foresters oversee Shasta and Trinity lakes.

The shores of Trinity (Clair Engle) Lake are less developed than those around Shasta Lake. Lying at the base of the Trinity Alps—in some places within five miles of the wilderness boundary—Trinity Lake and downstream Lewiston Lake reflect 8,091-foot Granite Peak, 7,929-foot Red Mountain, and 7,596-foot Ycatapom Peak.

Trinity Lake's wooded shores shelter eighteen campgrounds, five boat ramps, four resort marinas, four picnic areas, and swimming beaches—all in six of the lakes' twenty-one big arms. Trinity Lake is popular with boaters and water skiers. Lewiston Lake appeals to fishermen who catch rainbow, brown, and brook trout.

Each of the three units of the 203,587-acre Whiskeytown-Shasta-Trinity National Recreation Area has a different watersport draw. Waterskiers often congregate on the McCloud River and Sacramento River arms of Shasta Lake, top right.   WILLIAM LLOYD

At 602 feet, Shasta Dam, bottom right, is the second largest concrete dam in the United States. The dam traps water from the McCloud, Pit, Squaw, and Sacramento rivers, creating a 30,000-acre lake at its fullest.
ED COOPER

Eleven marinas scattered around Shasta Lake, left, rent houseboats, fishing and ski boats, and sell fuel and supplies. Foresters maintain campgrounds on the wooded shores, including some that can be reached only by boat.   JEFF GNASS

These lakes flooded old mines and towns. Founded in 1851, the village of Trinity Center moved late in that decade to make way for expanded gold mining, then moved again in 1959 when Trinity Dam and Trinity Lake were added to the Central Valley Project. Periodic droughts drop the lake to unusually low levels, exposing thirty-foot piles of boulders that were tailing piles from hydraulic dredges. The powerful dredges worked the bed of the Trinity River near the turn of the century to extract gold—two thousand ounces in one legendary ten-day span.

On the southern flank of the Shasta-Trinity National Forest, undammed water runs on the South Fork Trinity River, a wild and scenic rivers. These lands are sparsely populated and heavily logged, save for the small Chanchelulla Wilderness and large Yolla Bolly-Middle Eel Wilderness.

The Yolla Bolly area also marks the southern end of the Klamath Mountains. The mountain ranges here—the Salmons and the Trinities—twist and turn from east-west ridges toward north-south ridges, further evidence of the dynamic forces that shaped the contours of Shasta-Trinity National Forest. ∎

A swallowtail butterfly lights on a blossoming larkspur, absorbing sunlight as it readies for a day's journey.
DAVID CAVAGNARO

MOUNTAIN OF MYTH AND MAJESTY

"Before there were people on the earth, the Chief of the Sky Spirits grew tired of his home in the Above World, because the air was always brittle with an icy cold. So he carved a hole in the sky with a stone and pushed all the snow and ice down below until he made a great mound that reached from earth almost to the sky."

So says Modoc Indian legend about the creation of Mt. Shasta in Shasta-Trinity National Forest. The myth also says the Sky Spirit was so enamored of his work that he moved his family from the heavens to live inside the snowy mound. The family's fires explained the smoking volcano—when the Sky Spirit threw another log on the fire, sparks would fly and the earth would tremble.

The Sky Spirit created more than the mountain. Wherever he poked his finger in the snow, a tree grew. Rivers and lakes formed in his footsteps. He broke his walking stick and scattered the pieces, which became otter, beaver, fish—and the great grizzly bear, which originally walked on two feet, as people do.

One day, a strong gust of wind blew the Sky Spirit's young daughter to the base of the mountain. There she was raised by a family of grizzlies, eventually marrying the eldest son and begetting strange children by him. The Sky Spirit was not pleased with his grandchildren, and he was angry at the grizzlies for not returning his daughter to him when she was young, so he banished all grizzlies to walk forever on all fours.

Scientists have different—though no less fantastic—explanations for Mt. Shasta. The mountain is a composite of four volcanoes that began erupting several million years ago, spewing and spilling lava across a wide area.

Mt. Shasta is the highest Cascade Mountain in California and the second highest in the Cascade Range—trailing only 14,406-foot Mt. Rainier. The Cascades are active volcanoes—as shown by the eruption of Mt. St. Helens in 1980. Mt. Shasta is classified as active, although it may not have erupted since a 16th century French explorer recorded seeing a volcano spew smoke and ash as he sailed along the coast.

The glacier-clad mountain lures five thousand climbers each year. The most challenging of sixteen established routes ascend the north and northeast faces. The easiest and most popular routes are on the south faces. Climbers should file their climbing plan at the Mt. Shasta Ranger Station. The mountain claims at least one life a year.

In the winter, nordic ski tours are popular in the meadows, while alpine skiing takes place at the Mt. Shasta Ski Park. A new ski resort is scheduled to open in the early 1990s.

One of sixteen routes to Shasta's summit, this ascent up Whitney Glacier is considered straightforward but arduous. JON GNASS

FIREFIGHTERS ON CALL

Every summer—earlier in drought years—they arrive, forty men and women who spend the next thirteen weeks jumping from low-flying airplanes into forest fires no one else can control.

The smoke jumpers are an elite corps with a part-time job so sought after there is a waiting list. It's a frenetic job. Calls to scramble come in bunches. Firefighters must be airborne in five minutes. And jump from 1,500 feet to within a quarter-mile of a raging fire. And then, with one or more partners, use a "misery whip," the legendary six-foot cross-cut saw, a chain saw, and a pulaski to hand-cut a fire line. With that job finished, each firefighter lugs 120 pounds of equipment several miles to a rendezvous point for the flight back to Redding—or to another fire.

The smoke jumpers are just one facet of the Northern California Service Center, a military-style complex operated by the Forest Service and the state of California on the outskirts of Redding, near the headquarters of Shasta-Trinity National Forest.

The center coordinates air tankers, helicopters, dozens of fire crews, and tons of equipment and supplies to fight fires on state and national forest lands throughout northern California. Operations expand to other areas in severe fire situations. When things get to burning, calls come in from all over the state and the western United States.

In 1988 firefighters dumped 1.2 million gallons of fire retardants from air tankers, above, stationed at a joint state-federal command center outside Redding. TOM MYERS

Fires followed drought years in 1987 and 1988, burning more than a million acres of national forest land in California.
ROB BADGER

Jeffrey pine grows strong and straight, enhancing its value to loggers as well as to the wildlife that rely on it for shelter and food. Drooping limbs help the trees slough off heavy snows that might otherwise cause them damage. JEFF GNASS

SHASTA-TRINITY
NATIONAL FOREST DIRECTORY

P O I N T S   O F   I N T E R E S T

MT. SHASTA rises 14,162 feet to dominate these national forests and the northern tier of California. About 5,000 hikers and climbers each year attempt the summit. The beautiful mountain provides numerous scenic views.

SHASTA LAKE INFORMATION CENTER provides information about fishing, swimming, boating, and sight-seeing in and around the Whiskeytown-Shasta-Trinity National Recreation Area.

SHASTA CAVERNS are eerie limestone formations, tours available.

TRINITY and **NEW RIVERS** are wild and scenic for more than 100 miles.

R E C R E A T I O N   A R E A

WHISKEYTOWN-SHASTA-TRINITY 203,500 acres and four large reservoirs. National Park Service manages Whiskeytown Lake. Forest Service controls Shasta, Trinity, and Lewiston lakes. The lakes are popular vacation retreats for houseboaters, swimmers, sailors, divers, and water skiers. More than 50 Forest Service campgrounds, marinas, boat launches, and picnic grounds are scattered around the lakes, as are dozens of private motels and resorts. Contact the Shasta Lake Information center for boat rental, campground fee, and reservation details.

W I L D E R N E S S   A R E A S

CASTLE CRAGS 11,000 acres adjacent to Castle Crags State Park dominated by sheer, 6,000-foot granite cliffs and spires.

CHANCHELULLA 8,200 acres of steep, chaparral-covered slopes and 6,400-foot Chanchelulla Peak.

MT. SHASTA 38,000 acres protecting the barren, unstable, decomposed granite of the upper slopes. Five glaciers, mottled and treacherously slick in dry years, cap the mountain and the wilderness area.

TRINITY ALPS 513,100 acres of steep, rugged canyons and lush meadows and glacial cirques in the alps highcountry. Cattle, deer, hunters, anglers, hikers, and horseback riders use the area in the summer; a few adventuresome ski mountaineers dare it in the winter. The vast wilderness also spreads into Six Rivers and Klamath national forests.

YOLLA BOLLY-MIDDLE EEL 156,000 acres in the rugged canyons that form the headwaters of the Middle Fork Eel River, between the North and South Yolla Bolly Mountains.

R E C R E A T I O N A L   A C T I V I T I E S

HIKING AND RIDING Almost 1,500 miles of trails open to hikers, horseback riders, and mountain bicyclists. Separate trailheads for hikers and horseback riders into Trinity Alps. More than 150 miles of the Pacific Crest Trail—sections pass Mt. Shasta, Castle Lake, and Trinity Alps. Sisson-Callahan National Recreation Trail follows an historic trail on the slopes of Mt. Eddy and yields views of Mt. Shasta.

CAMPING Allowed throughout the national forest and at 81 campgrounds maintained by the Forest Service. Check with forest offices for fee and reservation information.

PICNICKING Allowed throughout the national forest and at designated day-use areas on lakeshores in the Whiskeytown-Shasta-Trinity National Recreation Area, at Mt. Shasta, and on Hwy. 89 along the McCloud River.

ALPINE SKIING Available at Mt. Shasta Ski Park. A new ski area is planned for the early 1990s.

CROSS-COUNTRY SKIING Most national forest backcountry roads open to skiers. Mostly ungroomed meadows along the McCloud River, on Hwy. 89, and below Mt. Eddy, west of Mt. Shasta. Trails at Bunny Flat, Sand Flat, and Overlook Loop on Mt. Shasta. Groomed trails at Castle Lake. Wilderness ski mountaineering should be attempted only by experienced skiers.

WHITE-WATER RAFTING AND KAYAKING Wild and scenic Trinity and New rivers flow fast and strong in the spring and early summer. Contact Mt. Shasta and Big Bar ranger stations for lists of certified outfitters and reservation information.

SCENIC DRIVES Coffee Creek Rd. leaves Hwy. 3, passes lush meadows and 100-year-old ranches, climbs past old landslides, and travels a corridor surrounded by the Trinity Alps Wilderness. Ends at a private resort that caters to wilderness photography expeditions. Hwy. 299 loops and twists along the wild and scenic Trinity River, passing Lewiston, Whiskeytown, and Shasta lakes and traversing the Six Rivers National Forest on its course between Redding and Eureka. Westbound motorists on Hwy. 89 drive along the McCloud River beneath a canopy of old cedars, pines, and firs that occasionally break to reveal Mt. Shasta.

HUNTING California Fish & Game license required. Seasons on blacktail and mule deer, black bear, gray squirrel, turkey, band-tail pigeon, mountain and valley quail, blue and ruffed grouse.

FISHING California Fish & Game license required. Nearly 1,900 miles of fishable streams, including the McCloud River, which is a wild trout fishery and divided into hook-and-release, zero-limit, and two-fish limit sections. In the national recreation area, Jones Valley in the Pit and Squaw rivers arms of Lake Shasta are good for rainbow and brown trout, salmon, bass, crappie, bluegill, sunfish, and catfish.

OFF-ROAD VEHICLES AND SNOWMOBILES Green stickers and spark arrestors required. Allowed on many national forest backcountry roads. Popular snowmobile routes on Pilgrim Creek Rd. and Powder Hill Rd., which leads to Medicine Lake on the national forest's east side.

A D M I N I S T R A T I V E   O F F I C E S

FORESTS HEADQUARTERS 2400 Washington Ave., Redding CA 96001 (916) 246-5222

BIG BAR RANGER DISTRICT Star Rte. 1, Box 10, Big Bar CA 96010 (916) 623-6106

HAYFORK RANGER DISTRICT P.O. Box 159, Hayfork CA 96041 (916) 628-5227

MCCLOUD RANGER DISTRICT Drawer 1, McCloud CA 96057 (916) 964-2184

MT. SHASTA RANGER DISTRICT 204 W. Alma, Mt. Shasta CA 96067 (916) 926-4511

SHASTA LAKE RANGER DISTRICT AND INFORMATION CENTER 6543 Holiday Dr., Redding CA 96003 (916) 275-1587

WEAVERVILLE RANGER DISTRICT P.O. Box T, Weaverville CA 96093 (916) 623-2121

YOLLA-BOLLA RANGER DISTRICT Platina CA 96076 (916) 352-4211

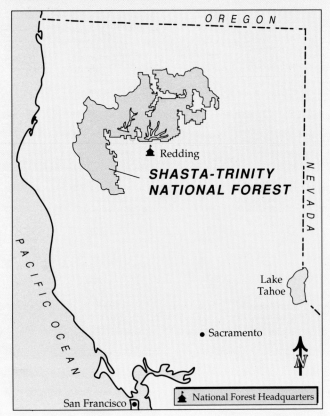

Nourished by heavy snows, 14,162-foot-high Mt. Shasta provides year-round skiing. This giant is 17 miles in diameter and towers 7,000 feet higher than the nearby Cascade peaks. JEFF GNASS

Lupine and goldfield bloom in the Mad River Valley below South Fork Mountain in the Six Rivers National Forest. LARRY ULRICH

Klamath, Six Rivers, and Mendocino

Wood, water, and wilderness

Tucked away in the northwest corner of California, the Klamath, Six Rivers, and Mendocino national forests are working lands that welcome outdoor recreationists.

These three national forests lie on ten mountain ranges that are a jumble of geography. An eastern chunk of the Klamath wraps around the southern-most portion of the volcanic Cascade range, but the main portions of Klamath and Six Rivers spread over several Klamath Mountain ranges—Marble, Salmon, Siskiyou, Scott, Trinity. Farther south, the Mendocino National Forest straddles the North Coast mountain range.

The mountains of Klamath and Six Rivers national forests are steep, rugged, and heavily timbered. In the past, loggers cut more trees—Douglas-fir, incense-cedar, ponderosa and sugar pine—in Klamath than in any national forest in California. Six Rivers regularly ranks among the top five California national forests in timber harvests. The northern portion of Mendocino supplies abundant Douglas-fir.

The three forests are contiguous, but climatic conditions change from north to south. Klamath and Six Rivers occupy the moist northern area. A portion of Klamath spreads into Oregon, and the northern tip of Six Rivers abuts the state line. From there, Six Rivers stretches south in a narrow band to Mendocino National Forest, where timbered mountains give way to drier slopes in Mendocino's southern reaches.

Climate influences recreation as well as tree growth. Numerous streams pour from these national forests into the Pacific Ocean. The waterways attract fishermen, rafters, and kayakers. In fact, the five hundred miles of wild and scenic rivers on the Klamath and Six Rivers national forests create one of the best white-water areas in the nation. In Mendocino's southern section, off-road vehicles replace rafts as the favorite form of recreational travel.

Come autumn, the delicate, urn-shaped spring flowers of the salal shrub become black fruits that resemble huckleberries. Most humans skip the bland berries, but birds eat them zealously.
JEFF FOOTT

KLAMATH

N A T I O N A L   F O R E S T

Klamath National Forest contains some of California's most productive timber lands, including some of the state's last remaining old-growth forests. From the volcanic Cascade range on the east to the Salmon Mountains on the south, Klamath is carpeted with Douglas-fir, ponderosa pine, incense cedar, and more than twenty other types of cone-bearing trees. The trees sustain a logging industry that pumps more than $1.25 million into the local economy each year.

One-third of Klamath's 1.7 million acres is managed for timber production. Another one-third—500,000 acres—is divided into five wilderness areas.

Each wilderness area reveals a different aspect of Klamath National Forest. Red Buttes Wilderness climbs over the sheared cliffs of the Siskiyou Mountains as they turn to run east-west along the border between the Klamath and the Rogue River National Forest in Oregon.

The Siskiyou Wilderness follows the west branch of the Siskiyou Mountains, rolling off the ridge that separates the Klamath and Six River national forests and spilling into the woods on either side.

Marble Mountain Wilderness encompasses more than ten percent of the Klamath National Forest from Buckhorn Mountain twenty-five miles south to Crapo Mountain, from Ti Creek Meadows twenty miles east to Shelly Meadows. Dozens of creeks and streams cut deep canyons, and almost one hundred high country lakes contain trout. Granite buttes and bald peaks rise eight

thousand feet above high meadows and lakes. The Pacific Crest Trail enters at Buckhorn and leaves more than thirty miles later near Etna Summit. Cattle first grazed here in the 1880s and continue to do so today.

Tiny Russian Wilderness surrounds 8,196-foot Russian Peak and Golden Russian, Lower Russian, and Russian lakes. Altogether, twenty mountain lakes dot the wilderness. Many are reached by the Pacific Crest Trail that cuts through the wilderness from north to south.

Trinity Alps Wilderness spreads into Klamath National Forest from Shasta-Trinity National Forest to take in the north face of the Salmon Mountains. Glacial cirques and moraines abound in the high country and glaciers still lie in the shadow of Thompson Peak, at 9,002 feet the highest point in the region.

Each of the wilderness areas contains hiking and horseback riding trails. One of these—the Clear Creek Trail in Siskiyou Wilderness—is a national recreation trail. It begins near Young's Valley, close by the junction of the Klamath, Six Rivers, and Siskiyou (Oregon)

Black Marble Mountain, right, slices across the Marble Mountain Wilderness in Klamath National Forest. The mountain is part of a shelf of metamorphosed volcanic rocks that appear in the wilderness. LARRY ULRICH

national forests, and meanders for eighteen miles with its namesake waterway, below Devil's Punchbowl, under Bear Mountain, over Wilderness Falls, until the creek leaves the wilderness five miles west of where it pours into the Klamath River. High country meadows harbor the highest concentration of wild lilies in the nation.

In the winter, cross-country skiers enter the Klamath to enjoy several areas, inclucing Scott Mountain, Carter Meadows, and Mt. Ashland. Scott is also a designated snowmobile center, as are Deer Mountain and Four Corners in the Cascade section of the national forest.

In the middle of Klamath National Forest, the Klamath River is halfway on its journey from Oregon to the Pacific Ocean. The Klamath, Salmon, and Scott rivers are the center of California's white-water heaven. Most rafters and kayakers run the rivers in the spring and early summer when melting snow swells the stream flows. Some sections are rated easy to run, but most are considered moderate to difficult.

The Klamath River and its tributaries receive fall runs of spawning chinook salmon and steelhead trout. While anglers ply the waters from shore or in drift boats, hunters search the mountains for mule deer, black bear, waterfowl, and upland birds. Klamath National Forest's good fishing and hunting attract sportsmen from all across California.

Drift boats are the fishing craft of choice on the Klamath River, bottom left, in Klamath National Forest, where anglers pursue steelhead trout and chinook salmon. The muscle-powered boats are durable and maneuverable on swift streams. RON SANFORD

More than 150 species of wild iris, bottom right, grow in California. These appear in the Mad River Valley in Six Rivers National Forest. LARRY ULRICH

Numerous cascades on the Klamath River, right, thrill rafters and kayakers. The Klamath is one of several rivers in Klamath and Six Rivers national forests that provide white-water recreation. DAVID MUENCH

SIX RIVERS

Six Rivers National Forest stretches in a narrow band along the west slopes of the Klamath ranges, from Oregon south 140 miles to the Mendocino National Forest. Throughout its length, Six Rivers rarely exceeds ten miles in width and at one point cinches down to a waist one and a half miles wide.

Only three roads cross the mountain ridges, but as the national forest's name implies, six major rivers— and dozens of tributaries—tumble down the mountains on their way to the Pacific Ocean. The rivers—Eel, Klamath, Mad, Smith, Trinity, and Van Duzen—are among the 1,500 miles of water on Six Rivers National Forest, including 365 miles of four wild and scenic rivers.

Klamath and Trinity rivers offer the best rafting through deep canyons and over boulder-lined beds. The

One of California's insect-eating plants, roundleaved sundew, right, unfurls its tiny leaves to trap small insects on its sticky filaments. When an insect is caught, the leaf closes around it. The unusual plant grows in swamps and bogs at high elevations. SALLY MYERS

Middle Fork Smith River, far right, cuts through the steep Siskiyou Mountains. Foresters and California Fish and Game biologists have built fish weirs and restored spawning grounds on this and other rivers to improve salmon and steelhead fisheries. JEFF GNASS

Smith is a premiere kayaking run. Foresters can provide lists of certified river guides.

The rivers are prime spawning ground for anadromous fish—steelhead trout and chinook salmon—and foresters consider the potential impact of logging activity on nearby streams in planning timber harvests.

Six Rivers grows enough Douglas-fir, Jeffery pine, and sugar pine for loggers to cut the equivalent of 12,000 three-bedroom houses a year. Much of the timber is cut on the northern half of the national forest, and coast redwoods are sometimes part of the sales. Six Rivers does not have large groves of the big trees—most are farther west along the coast—but the redwoods do grow in misty, damp canyons. In the small Yurok Experimental Forest just north of the mouth of the Klamath River, foresters harvest some redwoods to study the nature of second-growth redwood forests.

Humboldt Nursery operated by Six Rivers National Forest was created in 1962 to supply seedlings for reforestation projects on logged and burned lands. About 90 percent of the 10 to 15 million seedlings shipped from Humboldt each year are Douglas-fir sent to nearby national forests and destined for harvest in 80 to 120 years.

The woods also harbor areas for wandering. Six Rivers contains just sixteen campgrounds and a mere 205 miles of trails, leaving ample areas for cross-country travel. While some visitors go on their own, others enjoy a guided trip on horseback. Three wilderness areas—Siskiyou, Trinity Alps, and Yolla Bolly—extend into Six Rivers from surrounding national forests.

One of Six Rivers' trails is the 16.5-mile South-Kelsey Trail. This historic path follows a portion of a 200-mile trail cut in 1851 to bring provisions from Crescent City to the Army's Fort Jones. The Army abandoned the fort, and by 1909 commercial use of the trail—which included moving gold bullion from Mother Lode mines to San Francisco banks—faded. The Forest Service re-established the south portion of the trail in the 1930s to give firefighters access to the Siskiyou country.

A twenty-mile drive along South Fork Mountain in the middle of Six Rivers National Forest provides a leisurely scenic trip. The paved road takes travelers up steep grades and sharp turns to a high ridge—as high as 5,848 feet at Blake Mountain. Along the way, travelers look west past elderberry shrubs, glades of "blue goo," the serpentinite schist that is California's unsteady state rock, and out to the Pacific Ocean—the final destination of Six Rivers National Forest's cascading streams.

Anglers come to these waters to fish for steelhead trout and chinook salmon, and to find the peace and tranquility offered by Six Rivers National Forest, left. ROBERT McKENZIE

The Middle and South forks of the Smith River converge in Six Rivers National Forest, below. Coast redwoods grow in several nearby areas. ED COOPER

The southern tip of Mendocino National Forest lies about seventy miles north of San Francisco Bay. That's well within driving range for Bay-area residents, and Mendocino attracts thousands of visitors for outdoor sports ranging from hang gliding to scenic driving.

Mendocino welcomes more visitors than Six Rivers and Klamath national forests, but it remains a working national forest. Douglas-fir and ponderosa pine are logged throughout the national forest.

The Yolla Bolly-Middle Eel Wilderness covers parts of three national forests—Mendocino, Six Rivers, and Shasta-Trinity—at their junction in the Yolla Bolly Mountains. Although the high country is laced with trails, the wilderness is one of the least-visited in California.

The Yolla Bolly-Middle Eel Wilderness holds the headwaters of the Middle Fork Eel River and 8,100-foot Mt. Linn, the highest point in the North Coast mountain ranges. The peaks grow shorter as the coast ranges move south toward Marin County, and chaparral brush gradually replaces pines and firs on the slopes.

Many visitors come to Mendocino for quick day trips. Lake Pillsbury holds back the Eel River to provide water for irrigation and domestic use, but the 2,000-acre reservoir also serves as a popular boating and fishing lake. Hang gliders float on thermals above nearby Gravelly Valley.

Each weekend from fall through spring, thousands of off-road vehicle enthusiasts drive up from the San Francisco Bay Area to three ORV areas on the southern

half of Mendocino National Forest. Middle Creek and Davis Flat are staging areas for trails on ninety thousand acres of open land.

Mendocino became a popular ORV area in the 1960s, well before the sport hit other parts of the state. As a result, foresters here gained early experience in designing challenging trails that thrill riders and protect the environment. Some areas, such as Snow Mountain Wilderness, are off limits to ORVs. Other areas require ORV users to stay on designated trails.

Foresters use receipts from California's "green sticker" fund—named for the $20 registration tag ORV owners must buy every two years—to build beginner loop trails, groom paths from easy to most-difficult, erect restrooms, construct campgrounds, and restore some areas damaged by wayward riders. Most riders comply with the rules, and some ORV clubs volunteer to plant trees and other vegetation on damaged slopes.

Mendocino National Forest lures many sightseers who marvel at the diversity of the North Coast range. Visitors can climb quickly from the dry, scrubby Davis Flat to the snowy, 7,000-foot peaks of Snow Mountain.

In all, the jagged peaks, steep canyons, wooded slopes, and rushing streams of Klamath, Six Rivers, and Mendocino national forests evoke wonder from a variety of visitors, each seeking his or her own favorite place. ■

Sheep travel along a game trail, right, in the Mendocino forest. Sheep and cattle graze meadows throughout the national forest— including wilderness areas. Ranchers must obtain permits to graze livestock in national forests. MICHAEL POWERS

Open meadows and thick timber provide good habitat for blacktail deer in Mendocino National Forest, left. Deer are one of several big game species on national forests in California. MICHAEL POWERS

Increasing numbers of national forest visitors take to trails on mountain bicycles, left. Where bicyclists, hikers, and horseback riders share the same trails, a simple etiquette prevails: bikers yield to hikers and horses, hikers yield to horses.
MICHAEL POWERS

Bracken ferns carpet the floor of a pine forest in Mendocino National Forest, right. Vegetation within the forest ranges from moist groves of Douglas-fir in the north to dry chaparral hills in the south.
MICHAEL POWERS

AN ANATOMY OF A TIMBER HARVEST

One stand of trees may look like another to most national forest visitors, but foresters likely know the difference in age, size, and species of trees from one stand to the next. In fact, the different characteristics of each stand may have been noted five, seven, or ten years earlier as foresters prepared their long-range timber-harvest plans.

So how do foresters choose which trees to harvest and which to leave? The process requires a wide range of information from a variety of national forest specialists.

Growing conditions in each national forest are different, so silviculturists—tree scientists—estimate how quickly different species grow to harvest age. This usually takes 60 to 120 years in productive national forests such as Klamath and Six Rivers.

In old-growth forests, silviculturists use a point system, based on the shape, height, and girth of trees—and the accessibility of a stand—to determine whether timber companies would be willing to pay to harvest the trees.

Two years after identifying salable stands, silviculturists tell national forest wildlife biologists, archaeologists, soil scientists, and other specialists of possible sales. The specialists survey the stands to see how cuts would effect animals, erosion, and scenery.

The specialists and foresters then decide whether to proceed with the cut. If approved, foresters must decide how to take the trees down and out. Options include clear-cutting, which takes every tree in swatches up to forty acres, or using any number of selective-cutting methods that leave some trees standing. The public is notified of all possible sales, and timber companies are asked to bid on the trees. Winning bidders have a year to cut and haul the trees to sawmills.

After a stand is logged and replanted, foresters return an average of every ten years to thin out weak and diseased trees so that the remaining wood grows straighter, stronger, faster—and provides good quality timber for the next harvest.

SAVING THE SPAWNING STREAMS

Times are tough for chinook salmon and steelhead trout. Only one in 2,500 ever get to complete their life's mission of returning from the sea to their spawning grounds in freshwater streams.

Humans have worsened the odds. An estimated 500,000 chinook salmon ran the Klamath River before white men settled the West. By 1983, only 46,000 made the 150-mile run. Anadromous fish populations dropped by fifty percent since the 1950s—and ninety-five percent of the clear, gravelly river beds where they choose to lay their eggs disappeared.

What happened? Dams blocked off some streams. Erosion silted up others. Toxic discharges poisoned some rivers, and over-fishing thinned the populations.

Foresters, fishermen, and conservationists saw the demise and fought back. Free-flowing rivers became wild and scenic to block dam development, and wilderness designation protected sensitive slopes from man-caused erosion.

These measures were a good beginning, but forest managers and California Fish and Game Department biologists knew they had to recapture lost spawning grounds to save the fish.

Klamath, Six Rivers, and Mendocino fisheries biologists began rebuilding spawning beds for chinook salmon and steelhead trout on hundreds of rivers, streams, and creeks. On Six Rivers National Forest alone, national forest crews since 1979 have improved forty-five miles on

twenty-three streams. They have placed gabions—rock-filled wire baskets—logs, and boulders in the streams to break up turbulent flood riffles and create clean, calm spawning pools. More than 150 spawning sites have been improved, and salmon and steelhead populations have increased from thirty to ninety percent.

Current projects include rebuilding deep pools so more young fish can mature and return to the sea, removing unnatural barriers that prevent migration up streams, and collecting eggs for hatcheries, where young fish are raised free of predators, then released in restored rivers and streams.

With all this work, the odds in the future are bound to be much better than one in 2,500.

KLAMATH
NATIONAL FOREST DIRECTORY

P O I N T S   O F   I N T E R E S T

TIMBER HARVEST AREAS are busy sites that move frequently. Check with district rangers or foresters in supervisor's office to make arrangements to see a harvest in action and reforested plantations.

WOOLEY CREEK and **KLAMATH, SALMON,** and **SCOTT RIVERS** are wild and scenic streams offering white-water rafting and fishing for salmon and steelhead.

W I L D E R N E S S   A R E A S

MARBLE MOUNTAIN 227,000 rugged acres with nearly a hundred highcountry lakes. Pacific Crest Trail slices through middle of area from north to south.

RED BUTTES 25,900 acres mostly within Rogue River National Forest in Oregon. Boundary National Recreation Trail follows crest of Siskiyou Mountains.

RUSSIAN 12,000 acres supports 17 cone-bearing tree species and more than 450 plant species. Craggy, glaciated meadows and lakes.

SISKIYOU 153,000 acres contains old-growth forest and areas recovering from devastating clear-cuts before Forest Service took control of the area in 1905. Wild lilies abound in meadows.

TRINITY ALPS 517,500 acres spread into the Trinity and Six Rivers national forests. Popular access trails are on the Trinity side, but Klamath gives access to much of the 400-mile trail network in the area.

R E C R E A T I O N A L   A C T I V I T I E S

HIKING AND RIDING 1,165 miles of trails open to hikers and horseback riders including 800 miles in wilderness.

CAMPING Allowed throughout the national forest and at 30 campgrounds maintained by Forest Service. Check with district rangers for fee and reservation information.

PICNICKING Permitted throughout the national forest.

CROSS-COUNTRY SKIING Available at Scott Mtn., off Hwy. 3 south of Etna; and Carter Meadows, west of Scott Mtn., Mt. Ashland, and Juanita Lake.

SCENIC DRIVES Hwy. 96 follows the Klamath River for nearly 100 miles west from I-5 south of Hornbrook to Happy Camp, a logging town and port for white-water rafting guides. From Happy Camp, Hwy. 96 turns south past Marble Mountain Wilderness and out of the national forest to Orleans. Along the way, the winding road passes old-growth forests and timber harvests.

WHITE-WATER RAFTING & KAYAKING Some Class I (novice) runs, but most are Class III to V (moderate to difficult). Contact district rangers for lists of certified commercial guides who run the Klamath, Scott, and Salmon rivers and other waterways.

HUNTING California Fish & Game license required. Seasons on mule deer, black bear, quail, band-tail pigeons, waterfowl, and small game throughout the national forest.

FISHING California Fish & Game license required. Rainbow and brown trout in most streams and lakes. In the fall, anadromous steelhead trout and chinook salmon ascend the Klamath, Salmon, and Scott river systems.

OFF-ROAD VEHICLES AND SNOWMOBILES Green stickers and spark arrestors required. Four-wheel drives allowed on Forest Service backcountry roads. Three sites with designated snowmobile trails: Scott Mtn.; Deer Mtn., off Hwy. 97 northeast of Weed; and Four Corners, on Forest Service road 15 in the Cascade Mountains.

A D M I N I S T R A T I V E   O F F I C E S

FOREST HEADQUARTERS 1312 Fairlane Rd., Yreka CA 96097 (916) 842-6131

GOOSENEST RANGER DISTRICT 37805 Highway 97, Macdoel CA 96058 (916) 398-4391

HAPPY CAMP RANGER DISTRICT P.O. Box 377, Happy Camp CA 96039 (916) 493-2243

OAK KNOLL RANGER DISTRICT 22541 Highway 96, Klamath River CA 96050 (916) 465-2241

SIX RIVERS
NATIONAL FOREST DIRECTORY

P O I N T S   O F   I N T E R E S T

SPAWNING STREAM RESTORATION SITES at Camp Creek, a Klamath River tributary, and Willow Creek, a Trinity River tributary, illustrate work under way at several locations to improve spawning areas for chinook salmon and steelhead trout. Check with district ranger stations to tour recent projects.

HUMBOLT NURSERY north of McKinleyville on Hwy. 101 grows 18 million Douglas-fir, coast redwood and 14 other species each year for replanting after timber harvests and fires northwest California and southwest Oregon. Tours Monday through Friday. Call (707) 839-3256 for information.

EEL, KLAMATH, SMITH, and **TRINITY RIVERS** are wild and scenic.

R E C R E A T I O N   A R E A S

RUTH RESERVOIR Four campgrounds on north shore of reservoir, and another just north on banks of Mad River. Boating and fishing, county road 501, south off Hwy. 36.

TISH TANG Five campgrounds, two picnic grounds, four swimming and fishing holes, and a cross-country ski area along the Trinity River and Hwy. 96 between the Hoopa Native American reservation and the town of Willow Creek.

W I L D E R N E S S   A R E A S

NORTH FORK 8,050 acres at the north fork of the Eel River. Dominated by south-facing slopes covered in grass and chaparral, the area is winter range for deer.

SISKIYOU 150,000 acres with craggy peaks and fragile meadows on east banks of South Fork Smith River. Spreads into Klamath and Siskiyou (Oregon) national forests.

TRINITY ALPS 513,500 acres also in Klamath and Shasta-Trinity national forests. Steep, rugged canyons, lush meadows, and glacial cirques in the high country.

YOLLA BOLLY-MIDDLE EEL 156,000 acres of rugged canyons that form the headwaters of the Middle Fork Eel River, between the North and South Yolla Bolly Mountains.

R E C R E A T I O N A L   A C T I V I T I E S

HIKING AND RIDING 205 miles of trails open to hikers, horseback riders, and mountain bicyclists.

CAMPING Allowed throughout the national forest and at 16 campgrounds maintained by the Forest Service. Check with ranger stations for fee and reservation information.

PICNICKING Allowed throughout the national forest.

CROSS-COUNTRY SKIING Allowed on many backcountry roads; some groomed or marked trails on meadows below South Fork Mtn. ridge, off Hwy. 36, and at Horse Mtn. off Hwy. 96 near Willow Creek.

WHITE-WATER RAFTING AND KAYAKING Runs range from Class II to Class V (easy to difficult) on portions of the Eel, North Fork Smith, Smith, and Trinity rivers. Contact district ranger stations for lists of certified outfitters and reservation information.

SCENIC DRIVES Four highways—36, 96, 199, 299—traverse the national forest and all offer sweeping, curving vistas ranging from dense pine and fir forests on the north to hardwood stands and grass glades to the south. South Fork Rd. rides high along the South Fork Mountain ridge, with views of the Pacific Ocean to the west and the Trinity National Forest to the east.

HUNTING California Fish & Game license required. Seasons on blacktail deer, black bear, Roosevelt elk, western gray squirrel, blacktail jackrabbit, brush and snowshoe rabbit, mountain and valley quail, blue grouse, dove.

FISHING California Fish & Game license required. Chinook salmon and steelhead trout run in the fall on all six major rivers and their tributaries.

OFF-ROAD VEHICLES AND SNOWMOBILES Green stickers and spark arrestors required. Most national forest roads are paved, so opportunities for ORVs and snowmobiles are limited.

A D M I N I S T R A T I V E   O F F I C E S

FOREST HEADQUARTERS 507 F St., Eureka CA 95501 (707) 442-1781

GASQUET RANGER DISTRICT P.O. Box 228, Gasquet CA 95543 (707) 457-3131

LOWER TRINITY RANGER DISTRICT P.O. Box 68, Willow Creek CA 95573 (916) 629-2118

MAD RIVER RANGER DISTRICT Star Rte., Box 300, Bridgeville CA 95526 (707) 574-6233

ORLEANS RANGER DISTRICT Drawer B, Orleans CA 95556 (916) 627-3291

MENDOCINO
NATIONAL FOREST DIRECTORY

R E C R E A T I O N   A R E A S

EEL RIVER Two campgrounds, including one for recreation vehicles, 9.5-mile Traveler's Home National Recreation Trail, and fishing on small Hammerhorn Lake. At the junction of national forest roads M1 and M21, south of Yolla-Bolly Wilderness.

FOUTS Three campgrounds, staging area for off-road vehicles, miles of ORV trails used frequently for rallies. On national forest road M10, west of Stonyford.

LAKE PILLSBURY Four campgrounds, one commercial resort, one picnic ground, Middle Creek ORV staging area, and Sled Ridge Motorcycle National Recreation Trail. On national forest road M8 east of Potter Valley.

LETTS LAKE Three campgrounds, one picnic ground, and fishing on Letts Lake. Five miles west of Fouts on national forest road M10. ORVs restricted to national forest road in this area.

PLASKETT LAKE Two campgrounds, one picnic ground, and two small fishing lakes. On national forest road FH7, southeast of Covelo.

W I L D E R N E S S   A R E A S

SNOW MOUNTAIN 37,000 acres rise to 7,000 feet at East and West Snow mountains. Bisected by North Ridge, Milk Ranch, and Crooked Tree trails. Chaparral-covered low elevations to red fir forests in the high country.

YOLLA-BOLLY MIDDLE EEL 156,000 acres that spread into Shasta-Trinity National Forest, rise to 8,000 feet in fir and pine forests and yield views of the Sacramento Valley, Siskiyou Mountains, Sierra Nevada, and Pacific Ocean, on rare clear days.

R E C R E A T I O N A L   A C T I V I T I E S

HIKING AND RIDING 613 miles of trails, open to hikers, horseback riders, and mountain bicyclists. Two National Recreation Trails: Ides Cove Loop Trail, in the Yolla-Bolly Wilderness; and Traveler's Home Trail, in the Eel River Recreation Area.

CAMPING Allowed throughout the national forest except when fire restrictions in place and at 37 campgrounds maintained by the Forest Service.

PICNICKING Allowed throughout the national forest and at designated spots in the recreation areas.

SCENIC DRIVES Forest roads M10, from Stonyford to Letts Lake, and M8, from Potter Valley to Lake Pillsbury, travel through rolling, brush-covered slopes to conifer forests in high country.

HUNTING California Fish & Game license required. Prohibited in state game refuge, recreation areas, and ORV areas. Seasons on blacktail deer, squirrels, other small game and birds.

FISHING California Fish & Game license required. Eel River below Lake Pillsbury and Middle Fork of the Eel, upstream of its confluence with Bar Creek contain steelhead trout. Pillsbury has trout and sunfish. Letts Lake has bass and trout.

OFF-ROAD VEHICLES Green stickers and spark arrestors required. Much of the national forest, except wilderness and recreation areas, is open to ORV use. Use restricted to trails in some areas, in others cross-country travel is permitted. Trail networks at Fouts, Lake Pillsbury, and Elk Mountain.

A D M I N I S T R A T I V E   O F F I C E S

FOREST HEADQUARTERS 420 E. Laurel St., Willows CA 95988 (916) 934-3316

CORNING RANGER DISTRICT 22000 Corning Rd., Corning CA 96021 (916) 824-5196

COVELO RANGER DISTRICT Route 1, Box 62-C, Covelo CA 95428 (707) 983-6118

STONYFORD RANGER DISTRICT Lodoga Rd., Stonyford CA 95979 (916) 963-3128

UPPER LAKE RANGER DISTRICT Middle Creek Rd., Upper Lake CA 95485 (707) 275-2361

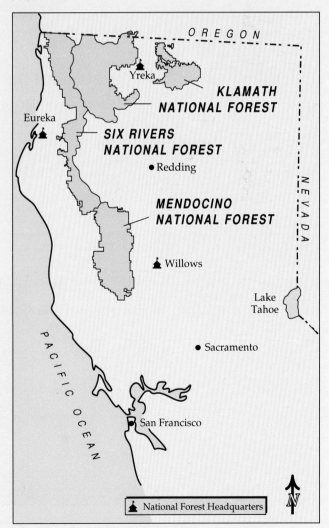

National Forest Headquarters

Cattle graze on the lush grasslands of the Santa Lucia Mountains in Los Padres National Forest. ROB BADGER

Conclusion

Forests for the future

"Californians have only to go east a few miles to be happy. Toilers on the heated plain, toilers in the cities by the sea, whose lives are well-nigh choked by weeds of care that have grown up all around them—Leave all that and go east, and you cannot escape a cure for all care."

So wrote conservationist John Muir more than one hundred years ago. Today, millions of Californians heed his advice and follow his footsteps into the nineteen national forests that cover California's mountains from Mexico to Oregon, from Nevada to the Pacific Ocean.

The national forests still cure most cares, but recreation is not so simple, nor so solitary, as it was when Muir and Gifford Pinchot, first chief of the Forest Service, together toured California's forests in 1896. Backpacking, camping, and skiing still capture the imagination, but increasing numbers of adventurers seek quick thrills on mountain bicycles and kayaks, and short retreats in motorhomes and houseboats.

These new outdoor enthusiasts take more vacations closer to home. They want to spend less time traveling and more time enjoying the outdoors.

In response to this trend, national forests are rehabilitating older campgrounds and designating scenic roads. They are creating more short, self-guided trails and are erecting more interpretive signs. Recreation specialists now ride motorcycles to manage off-road vehicle use, and others try to resolve complaints between mountain bicyclists and hikers, who often don't want to share the same trails.

The hiker-bicyclists conflict illustrates one wave of the

future in national forests. As more people come to think of each national forest lake, trail, camp, or plot as their own, they sometimes seek to exclude others who do not share the same values. In addition to recreationists, the conflict arises between cattle and sheep ranchers and wildlife managers over meadows, and between lumber companies and small towns over proposed logging areas. Often, members of one group believe the others are out to destroy "their" national forest.

The Forest Service tries to put the sometimes shrill debates in perspective. In most every case, the Forest Service rejects the notion of separate national forests for separate interests. Although they cover twenty million acres, the national forests in California are too small to divide into exclusive plots. What's more, the lands belong to all, and the Forest Service manages the woods to benefit the whole nation, not one group or another.

Few conflicts are likely to arise from a program to install wheelchair-accessible picnic tables, camp sites, trails, and fishing spots. Some visitors' centers now have programs for the blind. Others offer cassette tapes that guide drivers on day-long tours through the national forest.

New alpine ski resorts are proposed for Mammoth Lakes in Inyo National Forest, the Peppermint area in Sequoia National Forest, and Mt. Shasta in Shasta-Trinity National Forest. As nordic skiing becomes more popular, high country resort operators expand the number of groomed trails.

At the same time, backpackers and others push for more wilderness areas. About 444,000 more acres of remote, roadless land could join the 3.9 million acres now designated as wilderness areas in California national forests if current proposals become law. Another seventy-four miles on twenty rivers might be added to the 1,800 miles of wild and scenic rivers.

National forest recreation specialists estimate many little-used areas could accommodate twice as many visitors as they now receive. Other

areas—Mt. Whitney, Mt. Shasta, the John Muir, Ansel Adams, and Desolation wilderness areas, and San Gabriel Canyon—are so heavily used that visitors must be limited.

More lands will be put up for timber sales. Nearly a quarter of California's national forests already provide timber, but as old-growth stands on private forests are depleted, loggers look for more timber from the national forests.

The Forest Service must decide how best to balance logging and other forest uses, and it must decide the best way to cut trees in logging areas. Since the 1960s, clear-cutting in patches of forty acres or less has gained favor with timber companies and the Forest Service as the least expensive, most easily managed harvesting method that maintains a sustained yield of wood products for future generations. Selective cutting, which leaves some trees in a stand, is more expensive but less noticeable in highly scenic areas.

To maintain scenic views, foresters are using computer models to help design more large logging areas on the back side of a ridge, or behind a line of tall trees. Selective cutting may be used on roadsides and near campgrounds and lakes.

More visitors require more support personnel,

Children fish in a stream in Sequoia National Forest. Providing a diversity of outdoor recreation is an important function of the national forests. ROB BADGER

sometimes more than the Forest Service can provide. One solution is volunteers who help with information centers, trail construction, and campground management. Changing federal law to allow users' fees in crowded areas would help pay for maintenance costs and improvement projects.

Charting the future of the national forests is a complicated and challenging task. It requires experts in many fields, plus the involvement and opinions of everyone who uses and enjoys these public lands.

Whether as a volunteer, tourist, or trekker, go to the national forests in California. Discover their diversity. Enjoy their scenic beauty. And care about their future.

HELPING YOUR FAVORITE NATIONAL FOREST

National forests educate as well as entertain. With books, brochures, maps, signs, exhibits, and self-guided trails, each national forest teaches visitors about its natural and cultural history and its resource management activities. What many visitors don't know is that much of this interpretive material comes from private organizations, not the Forest Service.

Interpretive associations are non-profit groups that work closely with the national forests to provide many interpretive services. Some association members staff visitor centers and information booths. These volunteers answer questions, hand out forest information, and sell books. Revenue from book sales pays for interpretive projects.

Faced with budget constraints and limited personnel, the Forest Service might have to skip some of these projects without the help of the interpretive associations. If you would like find out more about these groups—or volunteer to help your favorite national forest—contact the following organizations:

Big Santa Anita Historical Society
(Angeles National Forest)
7 North 5th Avenue
Arcadia, CA 91006
Phone: 818-359-5511

San Gabriel Mountains Interpretive Association
(Angeles National Forest)

P.O. Box 1216
Wrightwood, CA 92397
Phone: 619-249-6754

San Gorgonio Interpretive Association
(San Bernardino National Forest)
4296 Mt. View Ave.
San Bernardino, CA 92407
Phone: 714-882-7233

Big Bear Friends of the Forest
(San Bernardino National Forest)
P.O. Box 2860
Big Bear Lake, CA 92315
Phone: 714-866-4607

Rim of the World Interpretive Association
(San Bernardino National Forest)
P.O. Box 1958
Lake Arrowhead, CA 92352
Phone: 714-337-2824

Laguna Mountain Volunteer Association
(Cleveland National Forest)
3348 Alpine Blvd.
Alpine, CA 92001
Phone: 619-445-5587

Eastern Sierra Interpretive Association
(Inyo, Toiyabe, and Lake Tahoe Basin National Forests)
P.O. Box R
Lone Pine, CA 93545
Phone: 619-876-5324

Los Padres Interpretive Association
(Los Padres National Forest)
P.O. Box 3502

Santa Barbara, CA 93130
Phone: 805-962-9730

Big Sur Natural History Association
(Los Padres National Forest)
P.O. Box 189
Big Sur, CA 93920
Phone: 408-607-2315

Three-Forests Interpretive Association
(Sequoia, Sierra, and Stanislaus National Forests)
13098 East Wiregrass Lane
Clovis, CA 93612
Phone: 209-299-4017

Eldorado National Forest Interpretive Association
(Eldorado National Forest)
3070 Camino Heights Drive
Camino, CA 95709
Phone: 916-677-2452

Southwest Parks & Monuments Association
(Shasta-Trinity National Forest)
221 North Court Ave.
Tucson, AZ 85701
Phone: 602-622-1990

Pacific Northwest National Parks and Forests Association
(Shasta-Trinity National Forest)
83 S. King Street, Suite 212,
Seattle, WA 98104
Phone: 206-442-7958

Loomis Museum Association
(Lassen National Forest)
Lassen Volcanic National Park
P.O. Box 100
Mineral, CA 96063-0100
Phone: 916-595-4444

A fisherman in peaceful Bald Rock Canyon on the Middle Fork of the Feather River, Plumas National Forest, tries his luck on an August afternoon. JEFF GNASS

NATIONAL FORESTS & NATIONAL PARKS—THE DIFFERENCE

Although different in many ways, national forests and national parks share certain characteristics. They both contain beautiful scenery and abundant wildlife, developed areas and wilderness areas. And they both offer many types of outdoor recreation. However, national forests permit many activities that national parks prohibit.

National forests began in 1891 as forest reserves managed by the Department of the Interior. The reserves were established to protect public land from fires and uncontrolled logging and grazing. In 1905, Congress transferred the reserves to the Department of Agriculture and created the Forest Service to manage these lands. In 1907, all forest reserves became national forests, and more national forests have been established since then.

National forests serve many purposes, including balanced resource development. National forests provide timber, minerals, forage for livestock, hydroelectric power, and water for domestic and industrial use. These activities usually are prohibited in national parks.

At the same time, national forests offer a greater variety of outdoor recreation than national parks. In addition to hiking, camping, picnicking, fishing, and boating—activities also found in national parks—national forests allow hunting, mountain bicycling, off-road vehicle driving, and even berry picking. Nearly all downhill ski areas are located on national forests, including famous resorts such as Aspen and Vail in Colorado and Mammoth Mountain and Heavenly Valley in California. This variety of outdoor recreation cannot be matched by any other land management agency. As a result, more than twice as many people visit national forests as national parks.

National parks were created to preserve certain outstanding areas in their natural condition, and only limited development is allowed. They are administered by the National Park Service in the Department of the Interior. The first national park, Yellowstone, was established in 1872. Today, Yellowstone is surrounded by seven national forests.

Two other agencies also manage large areas of public land. The Bureau of Land Management oversees extensive areas in the West, especially grazing lands. The U.S. Fish and Wildlife Service manages wildlife refuges, game ranges, and waterfowl areas.

Together, these agencies manage America's priceless outdoor heritage.

RESERVE A CAMPSITE IN A CALIFORNIA NATIONAL FOREST

Many of the major campgrounds operated by the Forest Service and the Forest Service concessionaires in California national forests can be reserved through MISTIX reservation company by calling 1-800-283-CAMP from 9 a.m. to 6 p.m. Monday through Friday, and from 9 a.m. to 2 p.m. Saturday and Sunday. Family campsites can be reserved up to 120 days in advance, and group sites up to 360 days in advance. Persons with valid Golden Age Passports or Golden Access Passports are entitled to a fifty percent discount on family sites upon presentation of the passport serial number to MISTIX at the time the reservation is made. Credit cards and personal checks are accepted for payment.

Not all national forest campgrounds are on the reservation system. Contact the individual national forest to find out about first-come, first-serve camping sites. For more information, contact the USDA Forest Service, 630 Sansome St., San Francisco, CA 94111, phone 415-556-0122.

128